ROMANTIC EGOTIST

An Unauthorised Biography of
JACK TREVOR STORY

BY

Brian Darwent

ROMANTIC EGOTIST

Copyright © Brian Darwent 1993

ISBN 1 85863 065 7

First Published 1993 by
MINERVA PRESS
2, Old Brompton Road,
London SW7 3DQ.

Printed in Great Britain by
Antony Rowe Ltd., Chippenham.

This entertaining biography of one of the most fascinating and complex literary and media figures of recent times is largely the result - factually speaking - of a collaboration between author and subject over a period of more than a year. Jack Trevor Story had no plan ever to write a straightforward autobiography, preferring to tantalise his readers with glimpses of a private life of bewildering complexity in his books and journalism. The very thought of a chronological account of his life in fact appalled him. His imagination was simply too strong and his method too undisciplined to allow him to think in such terms. But he was a very willing interviewee for this project, whilst having deep reservations, often expressed in angry letters - and persistent demands that the book be labelled "unauthorised" - about the kind of work he saw emerging. At the same time he could advise the author never to pay attention to anyone when in the midst of a piece of writing. This was the only advice that Brian Darwent was willing to heed. He has written his own book in his own way, defying all attempts to unsettle him right to the last.

Romantic Egotist opens with a snapshot picture of Jack Trevor Story in the spring of 1990, holed up in an old farmhouse to the north of Milton Keynes. The author then takes us back to his single-parent boyhood in Hertford and the fens; then on through an errand-boy adolescence in Cambridge, distinction as a young jazz guitarist, first marriage, a non-hazardous war, life as an instrumentation engineer in industry, children, girlfriends, a second family (with much frantic shuttling between the two), to his four decades as a professional writer. Author of such classics as *The Trouble with Harry* (filmed by Hitchcock), *Live Now, Pay Later* and *I Sit in Hanger Lane*, Story wrote around forty other books (if his Sexton Blakes are included), besides countless short stories and journalistic pieces (notably in the *Guardian* and *Punch*), film, television and radio scripts.

Jack Trevor Story died suddenly, at his typewriter, shortly after author and subject met for a final interview session late in 1991.

Brian Darwent is an authority on the Pulitzer-Prize-winning American short-story writer, playwright and novelist William Saroyan. In 1984 he edited and introduced a definitive anthology of Saroyan's work, *The New Saroyan Reader*, and is associated with two other posthumous American volumes. A mutual interest in Saroyan's writings led to his long association with Jack Trevor Story. Mr Darwent lives in Cheshire and is married with two daughters.

ACKNOWLEDGMENTS

I am grateful to the editors of *Staple* magazine for permission to use a key extract from "Cross in Hand". Acknowledgment also to Allison & Busby, Hutchinson and Duckworth for the use of several short extracts from books by Jack Trevor Story.

I owe a general word of gratitude to Jack's family for allowing this text to be published without challenge (the subtitle apart), and more specifically must thank his daughters Jackie and Jenny, sister Elsa and brothers Peter and Bernard and their spouses for help in interviews.

Finally, special thanks to Jack's old pen-pal down in Sevenoaks, Mrs F V Dunstall (Floss to her friends), without whose unrelenting support and encouragement the project might have been abandoned in the dark, difficult autumn of 1991.

Brian Darwent

Author's Note

To label a biography "unauthorised" whilst admitting that the book could not have been written without the full cooperation of the subject requires a word of explanation. Jack and I quarrelled a good deal during the later stages of this project, not least about this labelling question. He it was who was insistent upon "unauthorised", whereas I thought the idea rather preposterous and would not bend. It took our last bitter telephone conversation, followed by his sudden death, to bring home to me how serious he was. He didn't like the book and was damned if he would give it his blessing even as he fed me more and more invaluable information. His feelings were communicated to his family, who have asked that his wish now be honoured.

For Carol, with love.

The writer is a spiritual anarchist, as in the depth of his soul every man is. He is discontented with everything and everybody. The writer is everybody's best friend and only true enemy - the good and great enemy. He neither walks with the multitude nor cheers with them. The writer who is a writer is a rebel who never stops. He does not conform for the simple reason that there is nothing yet worth conforming to. When there is something half worth conforming to he will not conform to that, either, or half conform to it. He won't even rest or sleep as other people rest and sleep. When he's dead he'll probably be dead as others are dead, but while he is alive he is alive as no one else is, not even another writer. The writer who is a writer is also a fool. He is the easiest man in the world to belittle, ridicule, dismiss, and scorn: and that also is precisely as it should be. He is also mad, measurably so, but saner than all the others, with the best sanity, the only sanity worth bothering about - the living, creative, vulnerable, valorous, unintimidated, and arrogant sanity of a free man.

William Saroyan
A Writer's Declaration

CONTENTS

Chapter One

CHALK AND CHEESE

Jack Trevor Story and I have exchanged letters for years. I
sometimes wonder how it happened. One explanation might be
that from the beginning we could get each other's name right,
for we both suffer a good deal from having them misspelt or
otherwise garbled. I get Darwin, Derwent and Darwen, plus
an occasional Bryan, or Brain. He gets a hyphen between
Trevor and Story, Storey with an "e", John sometimes instead
of Jack, and the mistake that really drives him crazy, innocent
as it always is, plain Jack Trevor. Letters arrive for him
virtually every day bearing one or another of these renderings.
Had I not understood from my own sufferings that Jack Trevor
Story was a name you had to get precisely correct, our
correspondence would doubtless have been stillborn.

Story has tried many times - once on television - to clear up
this confusion over his name, only to receive sympathetic
messages actually addressed to *Jack Trevor*. He's seventy-three
now, so I suppose there is no hope. In the bookshops and
libraries you have to hunt through the William Trevor titles to
find his books. And even his full, correct name causes
confusion: editors reject factual articles in the apparent belief
that anything by Jack Trevor Story must be fiction. "They
think it's a *Jack Trevor* story," someone once said. Back in the
fifties he got letters addressed to *Mr Meynell Cottage*, the name
of his house. People don't pay enough attention, that's the
problem. It's one reason why readers have found his later
writing rather baffling. They need, and miss in his work, what
he calls the lubrication of cliché.

I first began to notice Jack Trevor Story's name about
twenty years ago, when he had a cult column in the *Guardian*.

I would have known then the titles of his two best known books, *The Trouble with Harry* and *Live Now, Pay Later*, because both had been successfully filmed (the first by Hitchcock); though I'm sure I hadn't read them. I don't think I used to read his stuff in the *Guardian* very often, either; not right through, anyway. I too needed the lubrication of cliché. Jack Trevor Story and I seemed to have few affinities. I couldn't have guessed that one day, all these years later, I would sit down to begin tentatively to write a book about him.

Our association really began one Saturday morning in 1971. He published that day a long piece in the *Guardian* that really made me sit up, for it was about the American writer William Saroyan. I had imagined myself to be perhaps Saroyan's last remaining British fan. Once he had been almost as famous and influential as Hemingway, I had heard, but those days seemed long gone. Certainly no one in my restricted circle had read him, or cared to when I recommended him. I had thus come to think of him in some strange way almost as my own property. But now suddenly, out of the blue, here was another fan - Jack Trevor Story. More than a fan, in fact, for Story was shouting to the world that Saroyan was his great literary hero and the inspiration of his own writing career. Incredibly, I had something in common with this strange Saturday-morning columnist who was baffling and sometimes outraging - besides of course entertaining - the smug readers of our best daily newspaper. The column occasionally provoked letters on the correspondence page, but none appeared after the Saroyan piece. Evidently the fan club consisted of only the two of us. I composed several letters to Story, with the simple idea of letting him know that I too was a Saroyan enthusiast (Saroyan himself I regarded as totally unapproachable), but none of them seemed quite right somehow. I couldn't claim that Saroyan had inspired my own literary career because I didn't have one, only the desire. I was in truth intimidated - out of my depth, the piece on our mutual hero aside. So I let it go.

Six or seven years then passed, in which Saroyan's books disappeared from print in Britain and Jack Trevor Story's name all but disappeared from the pages of the *Guardian*. I had conceived the ambitious idea of compiling a new Saroyan anthology and was casting around for a famous name to co-edit the book and help it into print. Who better than Jack Trevor Story, even if he himself seemed to have slipped from the limelight a little now?

Well, my book was eventually published in America (as *The New Saroyan Reader*), though without Story's help, for I had caught him in the middle of filming a new television series, *Jack on the Box*. But he did answer my letter - at length and enthusiastically - and in time we became regular correspondents.

That kind of thing rarely happens. Many famous people, writers or otherwise, will answer perhaps one letter; but that is as far as it goes. They are not as a rule looking for a pen-pal. With Jack Trevor Story, however, I found that the compulsion to answer letters was at least as strong on his side as mine, maybe stronger. Unreliable he may be in many ways at the personal level, but as a correspondent he can be relied upon totally. But the curious thing about our letters is that despite so many I feel I hardly know him. We don't really connect; there has never in all the years been a real meeting of minds.

I didn't actually meet Story in the flesh until the late eighties, around the time of his seventieth birthday. One of the problems was that his home is so very difficult to find. Members of his own family have been known to turn back defeated. He lives in an old farmhouse to the north of Milton Keynes, Stacey Hill Farm. That was as much as I knew in the first years of our association. On the rare occasions when I was in the area I looked around to see if I could locate the place, but never very earnestly. I imagined it would be easy to spot, standing on a hill. None of the farms I looked at answered that description, or had the right sign on the gate.

These casual searches were spread over several years, at long intervals. Why was I being so half-hearted? We were friends after all, in a manner of speaking. But writers for me existed somehow in another dimension. I didn't know any outside their books, had never even seen one. I was a little scared to cross what I felt to be a metaphysical barrier of some sort. Nevertheless, one day at last I bought a map of Milton Keynes. Only then did I discover that Stacey Hill Farm was part of a kind of museum complex - a "Collection of Industrial and Rural Life". And even with the benefit of the map you had to search for it, for the establishment then lacked a sign. But at last one spring afternoon I drove slowly onto the gravel in front of the old farmhouse and rang the bell, an unexpected visitor.

My elder daughter had just begun a four-year course at a university in the London area. We live in Cheshire, so whenever I was transporting her possessions from home to college or back again I began to call in to say hello. This must mean, you might think, that I am getting to know him better now. Maybe I am, but the truth is that we are like chalk and cheese. Our lives are as different as it is possible for two lives to be. True, we both have backgrounds in engineering (mine continues), both like to talk about books and writers in an increasingly illiterate world, and even our age difference is not so very great; yet we meet almost as strangers. We don't have the intuitive understanding of one another that you expect friends to have.

Yet in spite of all this the idea has lately surfaced that perhaps I am the right man to write Story's biography. Since he is a writer himself, and one moreover who writes most frequently in an autobiographical vein, a biographer is on the face of it surplus to requirements. But readers of both biographies and autobiographies expect an author as a rule to begin somewhere close to the beginning and then to proceed without too many digressions through the seven ages. This seems to me a perfectly reasonable expectation, but such an approach is utterly alien to Story. For him autobiography is art - his life something to mix into his fiction. Consequently there is not the slightest chance that he will ever write his life story in the straightforward manner, fascinating as I know it has been. That is a task for someone else. But why me? Well, one reason is that he can't bear sycophants, and in me he may have the opposite.

It is April, 1990. I have already done one taped interview session with Jack Trevor Story himself and have plans to talk to other people, notably members of his family. But as yet I have only the sketchiest knowledge of the events of Story's life. Like the reader, I will be discovering things about him constantly as the book proceeds.

The age of the literary pilgrimage is certainly past, but let me say before embarking on the story proper that there may be some around still who would wish to visit Jack Trevor Story themselves. It can be done. You will certainly need the Milton Keynes City Plan - and don't be put off by its multi-coloured complexity: if you make your way to the big roundabout straddling the A5 close to Wolverton you will be within a mile of Stacey Hill Farm. I wouldn't want to be more specific than that, since it is only proper that visitors should have to struggle a little to find the place, as I myself once had to do. But before you call on the man, a word of warning:

First of all Jack Trevor Story seldom has any money, so the drinks may well be on you when he invites you out to the pub. Secondly, he can turn nasty - dislikes being kept away from his work by pointless conversations, hates readers, and is quite paranoid about "straight" people in the lit-business. But most importantly, his life at Stacey Hill Farm is showing signs of becoming untenable, so that by the time these words reach print he may conceivably have moved out - into the home, perhaps, of one of his many daughters, if they can hold him. The unfortunate literary pilgrim will thus be left to contemplate the bricks and mortar of the rustic residence that through the eighties was the pleasant home of "one of the funniest writers we have" (*Sunday Telegraph*).

And now I find I want to begin by writing about Jack Trevor Story's present life. It may not last.

Chapter Two

JACK TREVOR STORY AT LEVERET PRESS

Under the small notice next to his door giving his own name, there is also a reference to "Leveret Press". This is hardly a separate business, however. Leveret is a company Story set up in the mid-eighties for the chief purpose of publishing the accumulating pile of novels and other manuscripts which mainstream publishers were increasingly unwilling to touch. They were to be interspersed with reprints of the famous old titles - and the best known two (*The Trouble with Harry* and *Live Now, Pay Later)* happened at that time to be out of print - the plan being that the money earned from the famous titles would finance the new ones. He had hopes, too, of bringing in other writers, in particular for an unusual associated magazine project, "Rejections". The idea was to print the *unpublished* work of established names, since this was in his view likely to be their best - that is least commercial - stuff.

It was a brave enterprise, requiring much hard work, but Leveret (signifying small - or perhaps short - hares) was hardly a match in the entrepreneurial eighties for the bigger publishers, with all their hype and funny money. In the event only two titles were printed: *The Trouble with Harry* (which might have been helped by the timely appearance of the famous Hitchcock film in the list of top-ten videos), and an extraordinary account of the break-up of his marriage to Elaine Hepple (a girl from the north-east about forty years younger than himself who had helped with Leveret in the early stages), entitled *Dwarf Goes to Oxford.* Story managed some radio and other publicity on behalf of these titles. In particular, he did a long interview on the John Dunn show in 1985 linked to *The Trouble with Harry*, and also attempted to promote the same book in a talk at the National Film Theatre. The novel revolves around a corpse which is forever being dug up and buried again to satisfy the twists and turns of the plot, the body suffering little cosmetic damage in the process. In his talk he read a modern and extremely gruesome story (that *Punch* had felt unable to print) which went over some of the same sort of ground in more realistic terms. This unfortunately went down very badly with an audience that had expected an evening of pleasant nostalgia. No books were sold, and indeed Story had virtually to flee from the theatre.

An appearance on Ned Sherrin's Saturday-morning *Loose Ends* programme provided an opportunity to publicise *Dwarf Goes to Oxford* - a book that was also extensively reviewed. But the result in terms of sales was less than had been hoped for, and the dream of his own publishing house rather collided with reality at that point. He still receives occasional orders through the post, but there is a good deal of unsold stock, now neatly stacked in brown-paper parcels in his back bedroom. Old notepaper - "Jack Trevor Story at Leveret Press" - is still sometimes used for correspondence, and he has certainly written at least part of one novel on the stuff, at a time when he was particularly hard up. This late effort once more to take the literary world by storm is typical of Story's remarkable optimism, which has survived a seemingly endless procession of set-backs and bad luck in his professional life.

Jack Trevor Story almost never bothers with physical descriptions of people in his writings. He says he is hopeless at remembering faces (this applies as much to real encounters as to seeing them in his mind's eye), and literally can't do it. (He is nevertheless an excellent mimic, both of speech and other idiosyncratic behaviour.) Journalists who interview him, and struggling writers who encounter him at minor literary gatherings, have no such diffidence when it comes to trying to put into words their personal impressions of Story's own physiognomy and other physical characteristics. Although these descriptions, particularly of his older and more decrepit self, can be disturbingly graphic, he is unfailingly amused by them. For this reason I am reluctant to try once again (for I have attempted it before) to find the right words with which to describe him as he opens the door to greet a visitor.

You may know his face anyway from book jackets, or you may have seen his photograph from time to time in the newspapers or magazines. If you happen to take the *Sunday Telegraph* you can hardly fail to remember a "beef-cake" picture of the man (late in 1989) illustrating a profile by Byron Rogers on the back page. This startling portrait is currently exhibited in a Soho art gallery, close to Samuel Beckett.

One thing you will notice, if it's the older photographs (of the younger man) you happen to have seen, is how much better his teeth look now. The old set, which where long, yellow, broken, bad and irregularly spaced, used to attract publicity on their own. (He once told an interviewer that the secret was to use long yellow toothpaste.) The new teeth are perfectly regular, by contrast, and as white as you could wish. They also appear to be perfectly serviceable, as you'll observe if you happen to find yourself eating with him.

This is unlikely, however: he is a regular eater of neither lunch nor dinner, so that his food intake is apt to strike one as scarcely compatible with survival. Back in the days of *Jack on the Box* (1979) Story had a noticeable weight problem. In the first episode he was to be seen jogging. But poverty rather than exercise has been the main reason for his subsequent highly successful weight loss. Slimmers, if they really want to succeed, should give all they have to the poor rather than waste their money on diet aids. During the financially draining Leveret initiative he was sometimes reduced to living on porridge. Even so, the man who opens the door to you at Stacey Hill Farm is not quite the under-nourished figure of the *Sunday Telegraph* picture. Whether intentionally or not, photographer Jillian Edelstein was responsible for that effect. Since Elaine's departure, Story has been seeking another (third) wife, and it could be that the idea was to offer interested females a nutritional as well as sexual challenge.

Behind the door are wooden steps leading to the upper floor on which he lives. Models of a Cessna light aircraft and a yacht used to hang in mid-air at the top, but they were destroyed in a recent fire. Despite a number of physical ailments, Story still climbs the steps very well. As you follow him up you may notice that he is very bald from the back view. Old photographs throw no light on the historical progress of this baldness, since they never show him anything more than side on.

Like many important developments in his life and career, the road to Stacey Hill Farm for Jack Trevor Story began with a pub conversation. A stranger told him of an Arts Council of Great Britain Fellowship, advertised in the *New Statesman*, for a writer in residence in Welwyn Garden City. It was to be the first creative-writing fellowship for a town or city; usually they go to colleges or universities. He was living expensively in Hampstead - the base for his cult column in the *Guardian* - already co-habiting with Elaine, then scarcely out of her teens. The stranger (a fellow author) did the rare thing of following up his casual tip-off with a phone call. Story learned that a £4000 salary was an offer, together with free accommodation. Along with forty others, he applied for the job, despite reservations. Thirty-five turned up for interview; Story was not amongst them. He had broken down on the M1. Such was his fame at that time, however, that the entire panel was prepared to stay on into the evening in order to carry out a late interview. He hadn't much fancied Welwyn Garden City, having lived there before, but that part of what the stranger had told him turned out to be inaccurate: the actual location was Milton Keynes. This was less familiar and therefore more attractive territory. He was still lukewarm about the idea, but agreed to travel up from Hampstead with Elaine to look at the various houses - there were six or seven possibilities. All were awful; one resembled - and perhaps was - a converted railway carriage. But there had been mention of accommodation at a mysterious "farm", which at last they demanded to see. They were told they wouldn't like the place, since it was run down, full of noisy school kids all the time - turning fairy stories into concrete under the guidance of an eccentric Polish-American sculptress (Liz Leyh, creator of Milton Keynes' famous concrete cows) - and with the din in prospect of ancient threshing machines and tractors from an agricultural museum being assembled on the premises that, like old Battle-of-Britain fighter planes, had to be shown to be still functioning. Story retorted that he had been happily sharing a flat with about eight other people and was in short well used to noise and disturbance. He liked to be able to whistle and sing and play his guitar, and wouldn't be inhibited in such a place. They still expected disappointment, but when they saw the farm and inspected the freshly painted five-room flat, with its marvellous views from the windows in two directions, they loved it. A farewell party was thrown for them at their Hampstead local; then with the help of a borrowed lorry they moved north to Milton Keynes in a single journey to take up residence, as odd a couple in conventional terms as could be imagined. The year was 1977.

The primary task of the job holder was "to encourage working-class writing". This was to be achieved by organising poetry readings and writers' workshops, and conducting more formal classes at a teachers' training college and a comprehensive school. Many of the region's aspiring authors proved to be quite elderly, so that Story sometimes had to provide transport for them, besides lugging their manuscripts around in his bag. One student was an ex-butler who had been close to the Profumo - Christine Keeler - Stephen Ward scandal and was shrewdly thinking of writing his memoirs, but focused ambition of that kind was rare. Most were content to dabble at writing, and needed encouragement even to show their work to people they knew. The thought of actually sending something to a publisher scarcely entered their heads. Story has more patience with novices than most literary celebrities, but this amateurism dismayed and depressed him, taking most of his interest out of the job. With his media contacts, he was very successful at attracting publicity - radio and television - to Milton Keynes, but rather fell down on some of the other requirements - writers' workshops in particular. He dislikes the word, and the idea behind it, and failed to organise any along the expected lines. Poetry readings, too, tended to be held in pubs rather than public halls. But all this hardly mattered because the job was only for a year. His and Liz Leyh's posts were evidently somewhat experimental in nature.

But the end of the job did not mean that he and Elaine had to give up the flat. The information that the accommodation would be free turned out to be mistaken, so that rent had to paid from the start. But it was cheaper than Hampstead, so as paying tenants they decided to stay on. More than a decade later, Elaine having long since moved out, there still appears to be no official pressure on Story to vacate.

Some years ago, a piece on Jack Trevor Story by Jane Wheatley in a series called "Obsessions" appeared in *You*, the *Mail on Sunday* magazine (for which he wrote a number of articles himself around the same time). More fascinating even than Ms Wheatley's words was a large photograph of the author in his study. The room then overflowed with books, papers, magazines, cardboard boxes and plastic bags containing yet more paper, together with a few more solid items, weighing down rickety bookcases and spreading from the floor and other horizontal surfaces up the walls almost to the ceiling, so that you wondered how on earth the lady had been able to force an entry to conduct her interview. Nowadays the same room is comparatively tidy, and something of a disappointment for anyone remembering that picture of chaos. He still spatters his walls with letters, photographs, telephone numbers, torn-off magazine or newspaper cuttings, and indeed anything in paper form that he happens on the spur of the moment to have wanted to preserve and display; but they are only single-depth now, and there are actually spaces in between. As to the floor, it is possible to stroll around the room deep in thought these days, without risk of tripping. This change suggests a partially reformed character, but in fact it arose because of the need after a long period for the flat to be re-painted. Re-establishing the old order - or disorder - has so far proved too large a task for Story's remaining energies. Even so, this is truly a room of his own, far more alive and interesting than any of the beautifully furnished personal quarters, with their little piles of carefully arranged coffee-table books, tasteful *objets d'art* and other exotic memorabilia, featured in the *Observer* magazine series. He is disappointed if visitors take no interest in his wall displays.

Other parts of the flat are moderately tidy, though it isn't easy for an elderly man (he is far from elderly in the mind) who until these last years has always shared his domestic life with a wife or girlfriend, and whose head is full of writing projects, to keep on top of the housework, even though he claims to spend more time at it than at writing itself. These labours suffered a bad setback one night (early 1990), when he returned from the pub feeling tired but hungry, put a match under the chip-pan on the stove, then promptly fell asleep in the bedroom. Only an accidentally open window above his head saved his life. Thick black smoke from the kitchen passed over his recumbent body - or so he imagined it later; he didn't of course witness any of this - and vented harmlessly outdoors. For days afterwards he was coughing up black phlegm, but otherwise appears to have escaped lightly (unlike the two models at the top of the stairs). The blackened ceiling in the kitchen necessitated another visit by the painters.

If you should happen to be a musical visitor, Story will very likely pick up his guitar at some point. The instrument is at least as important in his life as the old Adler typewriter standing ever-ready on his table. Playing it takes up almost as much of his time as the housework. He claims to be as good as ever, but doesn't play in a band these days. He likes to amuse himself by improvising endlessly on old jazz themes. His son Peter Lang was named after jazz musician Eddie Lang. His favourite composer and performer of the old days was Hoagy Carmichael, with Bing Crosby also a hero. Frank Sinatra he considers a singer lacking in humour. Back in the thirties, as a semi-pro, he won a *Melody Maker* guitar prize. But nowadays he gets most musical enjoyment from duets with his granddaughter Tara, a treasured but rare visitor who lives too far away down near Southampton.

Story claims at this late point scarcely to have a regular social life any more. His freedom of movement is currently much restricted by hernia trouble. (If your interest happens to be medical, he will treat you to a lively account of the journeyings of his lower bowel and his struggles with his hated truss.) He is rather dependent on people visiting him now, especially as the expense of keeping even an old banger on the road is getting to be beyond him. Not long ago he almost lost the use of his car (the current old banger is an Austin Princess), having been discovered by the police in a lay-by, asleep but drunk-in-charge. Only an eloquent plea by his solicitor, backed by a doctor's report, on the theme of how difficult it could be for a ruptured man to cope if things should go wrong when he happened to be out and about (no laughing matter, actually), saved his licence. However, at the time of writing the car has serious mechanical problems, besides being empty of petrol. But he is still able to use it in fine weather as a little encampment outdoors, with the radio on and everything. Visitors should refrain from offering to take him for a drive. He hates that. Driving has always been one of the passions of his life. In his *Guardian* column hey-day he burned up the roads in a big white six-and-a-half-litre American Ford Galaxie convertible.

Around the corner and onto the gravel might come such old friends as American journalist-adventurer Larry Levin (the subject of Story's early seventies' *Guardian* piece "Hemingway wasn't Built in a Day"), Paul McDowell (the legendary "Whispering Paul McDowell" of the old Temperance Seven, nowadays a television comedy actor and frustrated script writer and novelist), or - though rarely now - Bill Johnson (inventor and businessman extraordinary, the model for Story's best known character, Albert Argyle, of the *Live Now, Pay Later* series of novels). Occasionally too, Byron Rogers (a near-neighbour) might drop in; though more often they meet for drinks with Philip Purser. Then there are his more ordinary mates from his favourite local (the Crown in Stony Stratford). Most of all, though, he enjoys the easy company of the horsey little girls from an adjoining riding school, who quickly sense that for him there are few unmentionables and so feel no need to tone down the sometimes startling frankness of their natural chatter in his presence. This freedom of speech sometimes reaches the ears of guests, who despite progressive pretensions are apt to be rather shocked.

Stacey Hill Farm can nevertheless strike the casual visitor as a pretty deserted sort of place. The museum is still there (this is the "Collection of Industrial and Rural Life"), but it appears to do little regular business. (Story himself takes no interest whatever in it, even though parts of it are almost under his feet.) One feels that the Milton Keynes planners must be less than fully committed; that the farm itself, like the old position of Writer in Residence, is some sort of half-experiment. But it seems an appropriate enough setting for this late phase in the life and career of Jack Trevor Story. His own defunct enterprises (and I must here mention "The Story College", also listed in the address notices alongside his door) have failed in a congenial atmosphere of rural semi-failure, well removed from the distasteful, success-dominated business spirit of the decade now ended.

One of the worries in embarking on a biography of someone who is still alive is that important things might happen to the subject during the months spent writing the book, which could conceivably change the whole picture.

Well, I suppose the most dramatic thing that could happen in the year or so that I expect to be working on this project is that Story might die. God knows, he drops enough hints about the possibility, and in fact there are a number of real health problems stacked against him. He has suffered heart failure at least once, for instance - that could happen again. Then strokes run in his family: an older brother in Australia suffered a fatal one a year or two back. His hernia might become strangulated, or he might not survive the operation he needs, since a general anaesthetic would certainly be fatal and he has been cut about so much already that other anaesthetic methods might not be feasible because of the time factor. Not long ago it appeared that he might be diabetic, the main symptom being a disturbing tendency for his vision suddenly to fragment. Fortunately this problem was found to be due very probably to habitual aspirin consumption. He also suffers periodically from very painful gout. And over and above these maladies, he is now after all seventy-three. That isn't a very great age these days, but on the other hand you don't have to read far down the obituary columns to reach the conclusion that the seventies are not the healthiest years in the extended human span.

But all this is far too suggestive of illness and failure, and a misleading picture of Jack Trevor Story in the spring of 1990. Intimations of his own impending death may well be exaggerated. For the truth is that he is still in remarkably good heart - still optimistic. And professionally speaking, he could indeed be approaching better times. He had a very lean time of it with mainstream publishers virtually right through the eighties, but now suddenly his books have begun to be published again. The three Albert Argyle novels, *Live Now, Pay Later, Something for Nothing* and *The Urban District Lover* (Story refers to them collectively simply as "Albert") have been re-issued as an attractive single-volume trilogy, simultaneously with yet another edition of *The Trouble with Harry*. And all set to follow are *I Sit in Hanger Lane* (a reprint of the first of the "Horace" novels - Horace Spurgeon Fenton - and perhaps Story's most lavishly praised book of all), and a new novel at last, *Albert Rides Again*. After that are lined up *One Last Mad Embrace* (another Horace reprint), *Letters to an Intimate Stranger* (*Guardian* pieces), *The Art of Dying* (previously only serialised in *World Medicine*), *Brave Boys*, and four recent unpublished novels, *The Pensioner, Karen Radcliffe, Bring on the Ukeleles* and *Children on the Game* (computer hacking).

Meanwhile he is still writing every day (and through sleepless nights, too), limbering up his increasingly arthritic fingers with stream-of-consciousness letters, decorated with hand-scrawled margin notes and other personal flourishes, to his regular correspondents, before plunging into, say, a new novel (they take about three weeks), or a radio play, or maybe experimenting with a series of pieces to offer to a newspaper or magazine editor as the basis for a new column (which he would dearly like to have). His great hero and early inspiration William Saroyan made much of the fact that his first book was a collection of stories written at the rate of one a day for a full month. Saroyan was in his twenties at the time. One feels that even now, old and ailing as he may be, Story could match that work rate standing on his head, such is the undimmed fertility of his imagination. And he can still find the time, desperate as his situation sometimes is, to look at and offer sympathetic comment on manuscripts that aspiring writers continue to send him, sometimes out of the blue. The Story College was a brief attempt to make a little money out of this service; but he is no businessman. No writer worthy of the name can be.

So is it to be oblivion or glory for 1991? Well, going by past form, the most likely scenario I suppose is that nothing much will change. Reasons may be found for not proceeding with the reprints and new novels beyond the publisher's present commitment. More probably, knowing his sometimes awful bad luck (as an example of this, his prime-time, six-programme ITV series *Jack on the Box* was effectively destroyed by the first technicians' strike in television history), the manuscripts will be left on a train or lost in a fire. But whatever the future holds, it is time to quit circling around this aging author and his precarious lifestyle and go back to his origins in Hertford and the fens. There will be a more direct encounter with Jack Trevor Story's older self at the end of this book - all being well, as the saying goes.

Chapter Three

THE ONE-PARENT FAMILY

Letters to an Intimate Stranger, Story's collection of *Guardian* pieces published in the early seventies, opens with an account of a rather casual visit he made with his girlfriend of the day Maggie to the war-graves cemetery at Amiens to look for his father's grave. Jim Story had been blown to pieces in France more than fifty years before, but this was the first attempted grave visit by a family member. Unfortunately they were near to closing time and the woman in charge hadn't time to look the plot up in her records. "Fifty-two years and ten minutes too late," Story wryly remarks. The piece was an opportunity to indulge in biting satire, but that has never really been his style. There is plenty of strong meat in his work, especially his later fiction, but he has always been essentially a humorist rather than a satirist. He noticed that the grass around the British graves was much better tended than the rest. "That's because we've got the only lawnmower," the woman said, her voice musical with pride. It explained in a nutshell why the dead of different nationalities were lying there in their neat rows in the first place. So the grave wasn't found on that occasion; instead, since Maggie wanted somehow to see the thing through, he took her later to search for the Story without an "e" on the Hertford War Memorial. He remembered standing with the fatherless holding a poppy wreath on Armistice Days long ago, trying not to whistle during the two-minutes' silence.

Jim Story was twenty-nine when he died. There is a pieced-together photograph of him in *Jack on the Box,* the book of the television series (published by a small Manchester company, Savoy Books, who later went bankrupt). It shows a small, rather hunted-looking man with a youthful moustache, in tightly-buttoned uniform. Alongside the photograph is reproduced a message of condolence from the Secretary of State for War, acting for the King, which Story describes as a "receipt". He doesn't mention that the word "Dadda" is written on the photograph, though it couldn't have been in his own infant's hand as he was only a baby at the time.

Being by all accounts a good and kindly man, anxious to do his duty, Jim Story had volunteered for service at an early stage in the Great War. He was soon severely wounded and sent home - described variously as being full of holes and shrapnel, and badly shell-shocked - to spend a long period in hospital. Peter Story, two years older than Jack, has the most vivid memory of him then. Evidently his arm had been badly injured, and Peter can remember being fascinated by a hole in the limb, which he liked to touch. Jim Story had the misfortune to recover sufficiently from his wounds to leave hospital before the war had ended. Able to carry a rifle once more, he was judged fit enough to be sent immediately back to France. Jack's belief is that he tried to persuade his wife to join him in a suicide pact at that point, he so much hated and feared the prospect of a return to combat; but other members of the family have no knowledge of this. In the event, he got back to the battle just in time to be killed. When the news came Jack's sister Elsa, then aged five or six, believed that something wonderful had happened to her father. She remembers going around telling everyone, "My father's dead! My fathers dead!" in a state of great excitement.

Jim Story was close to being the youngest of the dozen or so children of Thomas Story, who owned a family business in Highgate. There was a photograph, now lost, showing the workers standing in the street under a metal sign that spanned the road. Business diversification is sometimes thought to be a modern idea, but the sign proclaimed to the world that these were the premises of a firm of Builders, Decorators and Undertakers. The Storys were a devout Baptist family, so that attendance at church services, bible classes and such was pretty well compulsory. It was in connection with these observances that Jim met Rhoda Dyball, whose father was also a religious man of sorts. They sang in the choir together. Jim stood only about five-feet-five, while Rhoda was close to five-eight, with a stately bearing and large bust and tiny waist. She must have been good-looking, too, for Jack believed for many years that a photograph of her that used to hang on the wall at home was actually a picture of the actress Lillie Langtrey. She would appear to have had most of the physical advantages, yet she was mortified when, having passed out during her full-immersion baptism ceremony (performed in adulthood), her stays had to be cut to allow her to breathe again, revealing to the world and her fiancé that her eighteen-inch waist owed more to engineering than to nature.

Jack once wrote in the *Guardian* that the Story business in Highgate had collapsed, and that his paternal grandfather had fled to Buckinghamshire to escape his creditors, never to be heard of again. This brought a swift rebuke from a previously unknown relative who turned out to be his Aunt Ruth. Evidently Thomas Story, a saintly man, hadn't gone bankrupt at all, but had sold his business and retired quite respectably to the country, owing to ill health. Later, when he moved to Milton Keynes, Jack began to meet or hear of other long-lost relatives. And he discovered that his Story grandparents were buried in a small churchyard less then two miles from Stacey Hill Farm.

His maternal grandfather was Sam Dyball, a lay preacher. Jack, who sees a close link between preaching and writing, might be judged in certain respects to be a spiritual descendent of this man. Dyball was an evangelist somewhat in the Elmer Gantry tradition, one gathers. He rode a tricycle, and had a reputation for bringing sexual as well as spiritual comfort to the newly widowed. His wife led the life of a martyr, for she not only had to endure the man's philandering, but also suffered as result of his insane jealousy. She developed, presumably through excessive childbirth, a badly prolapsed womb which made it impossible, certainly in her later years, to live a normal life. The problem could have been dealt with by comparatively minor surgery, even in those times, but Sam resolutely refused to allow his wife to be touched by interfering doctors. The result, as Elsa remembers it, was that she spent all her later years simply lying on a couch while her husband tricycled around, preaching to and comforting his flock. This, however, must have been a mainly Sunday activity, for he also worked in a tannery. Eventually he contracted anthrax, and suffered a rather horrible death. He had to be buried in a lead coffin, so the story goes. The official report said he had caught the disease from a bristle toothbrush, and it may be that he was forced to accept this version of the truth as he lay dying. Being dead was the only comfort he brought to his own widow.

One of Rhoda's strict-Baptist sisters became interested many years ago in genealogy, and set about tracing the family roots. She proceeded happily with the task until one day she discovered that the Dyballs were apparently descended from an improper liaison between a French duchess and a member of the peasantry. This Lady-Chatterley style aberration in the family history brought her investigations to a shocked end. Sadly no-one has since bothered to try to dig further into this interesting past, not even to corroborate the basic story as it stands, though Dyball is thought to be an anglicised version of the French *De Balle*.

In their relatively short married life together, Jim and Rhoda had five children. The eldest, Ollie, emigrated to Australia as a young man, where he died a few years ago, never having returned home. Next came poor Ken, who died in infancy. After that, at roughly two-year intervals, were born Elsa, Peter and Jack, one at least of the last two having evidently been miraculously conceived during the period when Jim was lying in a hospital bed, badly wounded. Jack himself is the more likely candidate for this distinction (born 20th March 1917).

Elsa has lived in a small council house in a quiet close in the Chesterton district of Cambridge for fifty years or more, thirty of them as a widow. She is a small, active lady with a sharp mind still. A defiant smoker (she claims to have better lungs than her brothers, even though they have long since given up the habit), she befriends and feeds the local stray or hungry cats while complaining that she doesn't like the animals. She supplements her meagre pension by taking in students, never in fact having enquired if the practice is permitted. Her life is pleasant enough, but threatened now by a planning redevelopment of her neighbourhood designed to cram more old people into the same area. At present the houses have quite large rear gardens. She continues to ride a bicycle, as she has always done, as the chief means of getting about, but has increasing difficulty with road developments that take no account of the needs of cyclists. The Thatcher government's gradual squeeze on state pensions is having its effect, though as yet her politics remain middle-of-the-road.

Peter, like Elsa, is quite short, and is thought to be in physical terms the closest to their father. He lives in the same part of Cambridge, with his wife Lilian. She is a religious lady, a Methodist rather than a Baptist, who rather surprisingly - some of his books are considered too obscene to be allowed in the house - takes perhaps a closer interest in the details of Jack's career than anyone else in the family. She keeps scrapbooks of his magazine and newspaper articles, buying them specially when she hears of a new piece coming out. Peter is a good painter, in somewhat primitive style, and a keen gardener, ever-ready even twelve years into retirement to take on any number of odd jobs for people.

There is also Bernard. He is the youngest of the family and lives a short distance away in Histon with his wife Peggy. There is a photograph of him in *Dwarf Goes to Oxford*, taken I think by Peggy, pulling a mock-bewildered face - supposedly after an in-depth discussion on Jack's latest book. He is very interested in law. But the important thing about Bernard from a family point of view is that he had a different father, as will emerge shortly.

All three of these family contemporaries (and their spouses)
express pretty much a common view of Jack nowadays. They
rather disapprove of his morals, but have liked (or sympathised
with) most of his women at the personal level. They recognise
him as being hopelessly irresponsible with money when (rarely)
he has it, and a bit of a sponger when he hasn't, but can accept
that his talent - and charm - qualify him for special privileges.
They are quite proud of him, though on the question of what
makes him tick - his ultimate motives and aspirations - more
than a little baffled. They find his later books in particular
pretty offensive, in as much as they can be read at all, and wish
he would sit down and write something that both they and the
general public could actually enjoy. And above all, while being
perfectly aware that Jack has always done exactly what he
wanted to do, when and with whom he wanted to do it -
something almost everyone else is incapable of - they find it
impossible not to like him.

But when it comes to Jack's childhood, Peter, Elsa and Bernard
are a good deal less clear in their opinions and memories. In
fact they have few really distinct recollections of that stage of
his life. Bernard was too young and Peter always too busy
(generally with arduous labours) to notice what young Jack was
up to. Elsa chiefly remembers that the family tended to do
everything all together, so that Jack didn't stand out in the early
days. And of course none of them had any reason to commit
anything of what was happening to memory since they weren't
to know that they would one day have quite a famous brother.
It may be that Jack himself, equipped as he was from the
beginning with a writer's faculty of observation and
assimilation, is the best guide to his early circumstances.
    Rhoda Story appears to have been an enterprising young
mother. With no husband now and a family of five to support,
she was soon running a successful tea shop on the High Street
in Hertford. Behind the shop, reached by a narrow passage,
was a disabled servicemen's club. Crutches and other aids to

mobility tended to be left in the passage. Jack has vivid memories of this establishment - of which again there was once a photograph, complete with explanatory sign - though his brothers and sister cannot bring it to mind at all. The limbless ex-servicemen played draughts and entertained themselves as best they could. To reach the place, those with no legs of their own, nor as yet wooden ones, had to propel themselves along through the pavement dogshit on makeshift boards. These truncated people had a disturbing psychological impact on the sensitive young writer-to-be. He noticed, too, unfortunates on the streets suffering from diseases rarely seen now, such as elephantiasis, and a perhaps related condition where beads of skin hung down from the forehead, sometimes covering the entire face. But he only became truly aware of these sad victims of war, poverty and disease later on, when they had begun to disappear from the scene. The horrors he saw in infancy don't appear directly in his fiction, though they may account in part for the sometimes bizarre excesses in his writings.

Things were going pretty well for Rhoda and her young brood at Hertford, when a rogue named Monty entered their lives. He may have had some connection with the disabled servicemen. Certainly he wasn't disabled himself, though he apparently had a minor disfigurement of the upper lip. He dressed partly in army gear, though this wasn't necessarily significant because random items of old military uniform had become a useful source of clothing for the poorer people once the war had ended. Monty Wheatly (or sometimes Malton) proposed to Rhoda Story and was accepted pretty quickly, the children (except perhaps Ollie) having been easily brought round to the idea with the help of penny bars of chocolate. She didn't know that he had been living with another woman, who had a young baby. On the day after their wedding, photographs arrived in the post of this other mother and child. But Monty wasn't kicked out at that point, strange to say; he stayed on with Rhoda, both as husband and business partner.

No one knows if they were ever legally married, though Monty evidently cost Rhoda her war pension, which she was never able to recover. She seems to have been aware from an early stage - and the revelation on the day after the wedding must have been all the insight into his character she really needed - that he was a con-man. He used an upper room or attic for storing stolen goods, and once even had the audacity to steal cutlery and other materials from the tea shop itself, afterwards joining in a police search for the missing items. Elsa believes that her mother knew exactly what was going on on this occasion, but didn't dare say anything. But she cannot in any real sense be seen as a willing accomplice. After a year or two she became pregnant again and sometime after the birth had to spend a period in hospital. While she was conveniently out of the way, Monty moved the children next door, sold all the stock, and vanished with a very young waitress.

Jack wrote a book about all this many years ago called *My Mother's Second Husband*. It was never actually published as a book, though it was serialised in *Magpie*, and short stories culled from it appeared in *Argosy* - as also, strangely enough, in a French magazine. (Was he worried about censorship - or family reaction, perhaps?) One *Argosy* story was called "The Night the Brick Came Through the Window" (clearly derived from a Thurber title in his *My Life and Hard Times* memoir: "The Night the Bed Fell"). One can never be sure how much poetic licence Story's supposedly autobiographical writings contain, but the impact of Monty Wheatley on his early family life was plainly considerable if a whole book could be devoted to the subject.

Rhoda's sixth child was of course Bernard, who is about five years younger than Jack. The fact that the Monty didn't disappear from their lives for good may have been because Rhoda was both enterprising and easy to exploit, as a woman still only in her thirties who needed a man in her life at a time when good men were in terribly short supply; or it could equally have been due to a belated concern for his own child's welfare. At any rate, Rhoda was unable to save the Hertford business after he had effectively ruined it; but then to everyone's surprise he came to the family's rescue in the nick of time by making arrangements for them to live in a very nice house out in Cambridgeshire, in the pleasant village of Meldreth.

But alas this salvation was only short-lived. No rent was ever paid, beyond presumably a minimum small deposit, and after six months of happy country living they were faced with being forced out onto the street. Monty had never visited the house, so it seems, while they were living there, but he was on hand when the time came to do a moonlight departure. He had now arranged new accommodation for them at Burwell, near Newmarket in the fenlands. The full family (minus Ollie, who had by this time left to live with grandparents, unable to accept a new man - or conceivably new *men,* for there are hints of other boyfriends besides Monty - in his mother's life), complete with all their furniture and other worldly goods, were carried the twenty miles or so from Meldreth to Burwell in a small, primitive motor vehicle of some kind, presumably an early type of pick-up truck. Elsa recalls that the children were tied with ropes to the sofa, but managed to make a terrific commotion as they trundled through the streets of Cambridge *en route* in spite of this restriction.

What awaited them in Burwell, in most respects a very pleasant village like Meldreth, was an extraordinary circular concrete bungalow with as yet no roof. It was raining hard when they got there, and the family was in some distress until a kindly neighbour offered them temporary single-room accommodation in another bungalow until such time as their roof had been fitted. In the meantime most of their furniture had to remain outdoors, lined up down the garden path, and was almost ruined. After the round building, with its dusty floors (evidently made from cement containing an excessive amount of sand) and freezing cold rooms (they all got chilblains), came what everyone describes as a "draughtboard" bungalow - so called because the asbestos sheeting with which these buildings were clad was decorated externally with a large check pattern. It was all very primitive still, with no running water, heating or adequate cooking facilities, but fortunately once again only temporary. Before very long Rhoda's business flair had lifted them out of the bungalows of Toyse Lane and into a small tea shop in a good position on the main street in Burwell, with more civilised living accommodation attached.

Monty had left the scene again during the impoverished bungalow period. One almost has the impression that he watched the family from a distance, and whenever prosperity looked like returning back he would come into their lives. Yet he may also have felt some sort of resentment towards them, as hard as that is to understand. He was thought to be responsible, for instance, for the brick-through-the-window incident, and other mysterious happenings, in Jack's story (this would be when they were in the shop), though Bernard disputes this. Rhoda's new shop was only moderately successful, until she had the bright idea - or a commercial traveller put it into her head - of installing slot machines. The year would be around 1927, and these machines were quite a novelty at that time, especially way out in the fens. From a business point of view they were a tremendous success - but this was of course the moment Monty chose to reappear. Wary by now, Rhoda set him up in a separate business. It wasn't long, however, before his influence began to have its usual adverse effect. Then came serious complaints, particularly from a nearby chapel, that the machines were disrupting the life, and certainly the churchgoing habits, of the village. The upshot was that they had to go. Predictably, this was the cue for Monty to go, too - and one can guess that he would not have left the scene empty-handed. The two businesses at any rate quickly folded, and Rhoda Story and her children were left destitute yet again.

Meanwhile, what had been happening specifically to Jack himself in Burwell? Well, he certainly went to school there (a state school, of course), as he had in Hertford and briefly in Meldreth. Memories of his early schooldays are not strong, however. And the very lack of vivid memories suggests that he had no particular dislike of either the idea or the process of education - much as one might like to picture him as a rebellious pupil, cleverer than his teachers and simultaneously ahead of them and bored by the stuff they were trying to instil into him. But that was William Saroyan, not Jack Trevor Story. Later he developed a considerable antipathy towards literary academics - indeed, the whole university scene - but he may well in the beginning have rather liked the idea of being educated. He admits to having been something of a sissy in those days - bullied even by girls - who cried easily and had little interest in sports and other physical pursuits. He had, too, a hint of asthma, and was certainly regarded by his mother as being the most delicate of the children. So becoming educated would have seemed like one of the few ways open to him of distinguishing himself.

But in the twenties, education for the masses didn't have the importance that it is thought to have today. Children themselves were less important. As to the notion of a career, that word simply didn't exist in the vocabulary of most working-class families. The primary social role of children, just as soon as they were able, was simply to work.

Young Jack's working destiny was assumed to be that of errand boy. "When you start work, make it Lipton's or Home & Colonial," his uncle Fred solemnly advised him, there being no need to specify what type of employment he should seek with those establishments. But that came later, when the family had moved to Cambridge. Already though, while still in Burwell and attending school, he was contributing to the family budget by working at various jobs (herding cows, for instance) in his spare time. And one of these first paid jobs was as an errand boy, for an eccentric chemist in the village. The extent to which errand boys were in demand seems extraordinary now.

The mad chemist's name was MacBeth. It looks as though he came to this profession, and maybe even developed his eccentricities, quite late in life, for when he eventually died an unexpectedly lengthy and respectful obituary notice appeared in the Cambridge newspapers, detailing a distinguished scientific career. Jack's main job for this man was to deliver prescriptions left at the shop. Chemists mixed most of their own medicines then, which would have taken time and hence explains why customers weren't inclined to hang around and wait for their prescriptions to be dispensed. And of course errand boys were ten-a-penny. Macbeth's old shop still occupies a prominent position in Burwell, though it has a different use nowadays.

His mad reputation derived mainly from a strange and macabre diversion involving unwanted cats that were due to be put down. He was prepared to pay money, as much as ten shillings, for these unfortunate creatures, and would send Jack out with a cat basket whenever he got word of one. The boy would be given bus fare, too, for cats in outlying districts. Macbeth first used to kill them (one hopes painlessly), then attempt to bring them back to life. The second and more interesting part of this procedure was achieved by rubbing cayenne pepper vigorously into the animal's skin. Anyone could do it, he would explain matter-of-factly, as though encouraging others to take up the hobby. No one else was inclined to try, but Macbeth's Frankenstein experiments were evidently pretty successful. His academic reputation was in the field of biology, so it could be that resurrecting cats was a logical extension of his earlier scientific work in research establishments. Alternatively, his passion for bringing animals back to life might just explain his premature retirement from academic life. It was common in those times to see pale, consumptive people sitting motionless in bedroom windows. Macbeth had a wife afflicted in this way. She was never known to come down to ground level. The conjecture was that the chemist's cat experiments had some connection with his wife's illness, though whether his plan was to restore her to full health or finally to dispose of her wasn't clear.

For a scientific man, Macbeth had other eccentricities, too. Religiously each week he used to enter the *News of the World* crossword competition. Not satisfied with a single entry, however, he would send in precisely eight coupons - never more, never less. That was his system. "It's infallible!" he used to tell Jack repeatedly, in his broad Scottish accent, though he is not thought ever to have won the competition. Coming by eight copies of that particular newspaper each week must have presented problems. They may conceivably have come into his hands as part of the cat-purchasing bargain, though that's only speculation.

One year when he was still quite young, Bernard came down with rheumatic fever and had to go into hospital in Cambridge, where he almost died. His mother accompanied him. While she was away, Jack was bitten on the hand by their small dog when trying to feed it. The hand came up like a blue boxing glove. Going to the doctor in those days could be a costly business, and there was no money for that. But at this point Macbeth stepped in. He offered to, in fact insisted on, lancing the festering hand - without anaesthetic, of course. This was far and away the most painful experience of Jack's young life, and the pain wasn't limited to the lancing operation itself but persisted for some considerable time afterwards. He might easily have died then, he now reflects with a shudder, for Macbeth would in all likelihood have looked on the crude operation as simply another experiment, his concern over the outcome having more to do with scientific curiosity than human compassion. But in the end both Jack and his hand survived, so maybe the man knew what he was doing after all.

Although young Jack didn't stand out from the crowd, nor even from his own family, in Burwell; looking back, those years have seemed to him to constitute his entire boyhood. Only when a ATV researcher went into the matter during the preparations for *Jack on the Box* did it in fact emerge that he had lived in Burwell only for about three years. At one time or another he has taken all of his women back to the place - though hardly surprisingly, they have felt much less emotional during these visits than he has. Even Cambridge - later - does not have the same importance in his heart. Burwell was Jack Trevor Story's special boyhood place, as Fresno was William Saroyan's. Such towns or villages will always seem commonplace to others; what matters is to have lived there during those special early days.

So it isn't necessary to dwell overmuch on particular aspects of Burwell that might differentiate it from neighbouring towns and villages. It is of course set in very flat country - that should be mentioned, because such factors can have an important bearing on a writer's later development. (William Saroyan, living in California's San Joaquin Valley, had a distant view of the Sierra Nevada mountains that he would one day reach or cross.) Only a short distance from Burwell was the Newmarket race-course, so that inevitably had quite an impact. Stable lads and other horsey people were much in evidence in Rhoda's shop (before it closed) and around the village, and the whole family were in fact at the time horse mad, as Jack describes it. Strangely, though, this did not turn him into a life-long gambler, as might have been expected, given his general readiness to throw caution to the wind.

Another dominant feature of his Burwell life was music. Scott Fitzgerald's Jazz Age was in full swing, and jazz music hadn't taken long to penetrate to the fen country. A short distance from the Story's home was the Premier dance hall. Girls in short skirts with low waists, and garters just above the knee, could be seen going in, and the music of the Charleston and the Black Bottom would fill the air. Jack still remembers the lyrics of all the songs by heart. Not much actual sex would be going on, but even so there was quite a heady sexual atmosphere for a hungry young boy to breathe, and altogether an agreeable feeling of gaiety in the air.

Rhoda's slot machines also contributed to Burwell's threatened slide into moral degeneracy. She was even open for business on Sunday mornings, enticing honest, God-fearing folk away from the path of righteousness and into what was after all nothing more than a gambling den - and one frequented, moreover, by the lowest representatives of that even more sinful vice going on down at Newmarket. And so there came the latest heavy blow to the family's fortunes, and the beginning of the end of the Burwell boyhood.

This time Monty Wheatley wasn't involved in finding the family yet another place to live. Nor did Burwell's God-fearing citizens come to their aid. The only accommodation on offer was a single room in the house of some astonishingly earthy neighbours. The house still stands on Burwell's main street, freshly painted and perfectly civilised now. Jack wrote about this family in one of his best *Guardian* pieces of the early seventies, "The Rapings of Dolly Foster" (a title designed to shock, of course). One would guess that Rhoda would have done her best to keep their room as clean and decent as possible, but she evidently had little influence on the rest of the place. In the story (said to be essentially factual) he describes these people as living in "one great appalling manger of straw and shit and filth". They ate from a communal pot, dipping their hands into the stew; or if they were eating meat from a bone, it would be passed round from hand to hand, each person biting off enough to chew until it came around again.

Yet from all this - "the miracle of the egg" - emerged Dolly Foster (a fictitious name). Jack himself has a much clearer memory of this person than his brothers or sister. He would have been just the right age - and the right sex, too. Not only was Dolly Foster very sexy, she was promiscuous as well. She even had babies. She was the step daughter of Sam Foster (fictitious again) - "a twenty-two stone cowboy". He had met

Dolly's mother and Dolly herself in Chicago. Then the mother died. In what circumstances wasn't known for sure - "sometimes she was trampled in a stampede; sometimes she was killed by Indians; once she died of starvation" - but she was indubitably no longer part of the family. Anyway, certain of Dolly's pregnancies were thought to be Sam's doing; but Jack's mother, for whom the image of the two of them together was so revolting and the morality of it so unacceptable, found it easier to explain to her children that the woman had been raped again - by drunken stable lads returning to Newmarket, or some other variant. Later it emerged that her children probably had different fathers. One boy was Jack's mate, and sometimes mortal enemy, Dicker Docker.

And among the likely fathers was Jack Carter (these names are also fictitious). He was a farmer. To have a secret private life in such flat country, you had to grow your own cover. This Jack Carter had done - acres of tall Indian corn. One day the farmer rode off into the fields on his motorbike, with Dolly Foster on the pillion. Someone with an interest in this urged young Jack to follow and see where they went. He came upon them lying in the corn. Story is good at these silent, time-stretching erotic moments, but the relevant paragraph is too long to quote. The silence was at last broken when Dolly noticed the inquisitive boy. She swore and shouted, while he ran and ran and ran - and never spoke or wrote about the incident for forty years.

Dicker Docker is one of the few people in his writings whom Story actually describes, albeit economically. He had a face like a fist, it seems. Obviously no sissy. Once Jack nearly lost an eye after Dicker Docker had attacked him with a club. It happened outside Macbeth's shop. But it wasn't from Dicker Docker, nor even his mother, that he got his earliest theoretical insights into the physical facts of life. His tutor in that respect was Kingy. Every neighbourhood has a boy like that - just a little older than the others, and always first with the latest sexual revelation. Kingy would explain all about how your insides would be sucked out if you ever went with a grown woman. It put into Jack's head a certain fear of grown women that has never quite left him. Dicker Docker was less of a theoretician; more interested in the real thing. One day (this is recounted in another of his stories) Jack was led by Dicker Docker in pursuit of some slightly older children, whom they observed up to early sexual mischief from a safe hiding place. Once again it was a moment of silence, with earnest faces and no talking. At last Dicker Docker, remembering perhaps something Kingy had said, turned to Jack and whispered, "They're playing dicks and bums." It's a measure of Story's beguiling way with words that he can make it sound as innocent as hide-and-seek.

"Dolly Foster" was provoked by remarks of a psychiatrist friend on the well-worn theme of children needing two parents if they are to grow up healthy. (Anger is the motivation for Story's writing more frequently than might be suspected.) The idea is insulting for those who have never had more than one parent in their lives, and also, he maintains, untrue. Single-parent children do not miss out; on the contrary, they have all the fun. Two parents usually have enough combined energy to keep children from developing freely, as they ought to develop; one parent by contrast is apt to be too pre-occupied with money worries and sexual frustration to be over-concerned about what the kids are up to. The result is that all the most vital childhood activities are the province of single-parent boys. Those from emotionally secure double-parent homes have to join the scouts for adventure.

"Scouts is chicken shit," Sam Foster would say, sitting while Dolly put on his shoes (he was too enormous to do it himself), before taking an assortment of single-parent urchins he had rounded up on an illegal fishing expedition or poaching trip. "Scouts is military. They're training you for the next war."

After Burwell, Monty Wheatley's effect on the Story family began to fade. Inevitably the opinion persists that he was a scoundrel. Every story has another side to it, of course, but Monty's version has never been told. His son Bernard, whose own childhood in Cambridge turned out to be far from happy, used to cycle to visit him at weekends; but even he lost contact when he was in his early teens. No know one knows what became of the man.

Chapter Four

CAMBRIDGE DAYS

Life had become impossible for the Storys in Burwell, living as they now were in close proximity to a literal pigsty (for Sam Foster actually kept a pig in the straw-strewn house, which he used to prod with a stick, from a seated position, to keep himself amused). Evidently Rhoda and her family had a separate entrance, but even so these conditions were intolerable. And in any case she felt there was no future, particularly for the boys, in the fenland village. It was time to move a bit closer to civilisation again.

Fortunately she had a lady friend in Cambridge. She had met this woman during her prolonged stay in the city when Bernard was in hospital with rheumatic fever (and Jack was suffering with his festering hand); in fact the woman was at the hospital with a sick child of her own at the same time. It emerged later that she had lesbian tendencies and was in love with Rhoda. She was also at least partly insane (not necessarily on account of her sexuality). She had a young baby, born rather late, which she several times threw across the room at Rhoda and others in fits of temper or frustration, the baby only surviving because it was successfully caught. Much later, the poor woman committed suicide by gassing herself.

But at first Rhoda's friend was a welcome contact in Cambridge. She arranged temporary accommodation for them in Great Eastern Street - off Mill Road in Romsey Town, a "Coronation Street" type neighbourhood. Once again the Storys (minus Elsa, who had left Burwell first, aged eighteen, to work in the Brunswick nursing home) had only a single room. But they were well placed to watch for other houses becoming vacant, and were soon able to move into their own place across the road. Great Eastern Street, a cul-de-sac, runs

parallel to the main railway line through Cambridge, which in
the new house was only just beyond their small back yard.
Famous locomotives like the *Flying Scotsman* would steam
noisily by at all hours of the day and night, thrilling the boys
more than they did their mother. Hard-working as ever, Rhoda
was soon taking in "theatricals" to help pay the rent.

Story uses the deaths of famous writers to fix certain dates in
his mind. One had occurred in 1928, while the family were
still living in Burwell. This was the death of Thomas Hardy.
The news was received at Jack's Burwell school with a feeling
of awed reverence, and not only by the staff. The word spread
amongst the children: "Thomas Hardy's dead, Thomas Hardy's
dead. Don't tell Miss So-and-so, she'll be upset . . ." Such
feelings in relation to the death of a writer are unimaginable
today, but in the pre-television, almost pre-radio age, writers
were very important people. Men like Shaw, Wells and Hardy
were the celebrities of the day, their doings much reported in
the popular press.

So the move to Cambridge had occurred a year after
Hardy's death, in 1929. Jack was soon established at St
Philip's School, also in Romsey Town and only a short distance
from home. And almost as quickly he had a spare-time job as a
tailor's runner, an occupation hard to visualise nowadays.
Evidently it involved taking cloth from one premises to another,
as one might expect, though the suggestion in the job title of a
speed requirement is more puzzling. It wasn't simply a late
afternoon or evening job. The boy had two early morning
chores to perform: cleaning the shop window and polishing the
tailor's boots. Since he was already up and about one might
guess that the tailor must actually have been *in* the boots during
the second part of this morning ritual. As in Burwell, school
life was pleasant enough, with young Jack continuing to offer
little or no resistance to the learning process. A major hiccup
in his education was about to descend on him, however.
Always his mother was concerned about his health. "He'll
never make old bones," was an expression she used over and

over again. Jack had a naturally pale complexion and a permanent look of anxiety on his face - as though he were carrying the troubles of the world on his shoulders, as one teacher not very memorably put it. The facial expression was in fact only caused by thinking about everything all the time; and as to his health, Jack had no concerns himself about that. But then a silly mishap occurred, followed by a mysterious and highly unpleasant bout of illness. He sang in Trinity Church Choir, for which he received seven-and-sixpence a quarter. This he spent on coloured Russian cigarettes (where can you buy those today?) as all the other boys did. One day he got the lighting procedure out of sequence and inhaled the match flame instead of the cigarette smoke. This caused him nearly to choke to death rather than laugh. The incident seems trivial but it was only after this happened that he began to be aware of asthmatic problems, and to notice in particular that he was allergic to sulphurous smells. Then came the bad illness. He was suddenly struck down with symptoms like those of polio or meningitis, and with no doctor evidently available to make a proper diagnosis. (His son, Lee, later suffered exactly the same symptoms, and that *was* polio.) Part of the unpleasantness of Jack's illness was terrible, ever-worsening headaches, leading to hallucinations. Someone would enter the room and he would see great gasometers bearing down on him, and other bizarre visions. Whatever the problem was no effective medical help was on hand; you had to recover unaided, which mercifully he did. Naturally, though, his mother's anxiety about his health had increased ten-fold.

The first thing she did was to bundle him onto a train and back to Hertford, where an uncle had a farm. He travelled in the guardsvan, aged twelve, with a visible label attached. The idea (or theory) was for him to breathe his "native air" for a while, as an aid to recovery. Evidently this happened more than once, and was regarded with some scepticism by his headmaster at St Philip's, who would announce to the school: "Story is off to Hertford again to take some more of his *native air*, while the rest of us stay here and work." While he was away his mother was busily pestering the Chief Health Officer for Cambridge to find a place for him at the Open Air School, where the regimen was specially designed to benefit children thought likely to develop TB. Before long her persistence was rewarded.

Elsa sees Jack's transfer to this non-academic school at such a crucial point in his development as having been a disaster for him, and something that he fought hard against. His own feeling is more that his mother's worry was not unfounded, though he recognises that it spoiled his chance of reaching the Central School, and thereby acquiring a Secondary Education - needed for any job that was half-way decent.

The Open Air School, which had to be reached by bus, was run by Leah Manning, a famous political activitist and social reformer of the day. Jack only realised that she was someone special, however, when she died (as he puts it) "on the front page of the *Guardian*", years later. At the time, she appeared to him simply as a homely women. He wasn't equipped to make a judgment on her intelligence, and the kind of lessons taught probably afforded her little opportunity to display it. The school consisted of four box-like structures, specially designed so that particular external walls could be drawn back to expose the working scholars to the fresh air. The weather had to be particularly foul, summer or winter, to permit normal indoor study. As much time as possible was also spent *entirely* out of doors. Each pupil had a "stretcher", which had to be taken out after lunch and placed in a suitable position on the school field, for it was a rule that the first hour of the afternoon must be spent sleeping. The special health diet included raw liver in the salad, cod-liver oil and malt (that would be a pleasure) and brimstone and treacle. Why the actual lessons couldn't be just as for normal schooling isn't clear. Much time was spent on handicrafts and art work. The results of these activities were offered for sale to help boost school funds so that might be part of the explanation. One school product was firescreens. A great early thrill for Jack was that certain lessons consisted of broadcasts on the radio. Leah Manning evidently thought it tremendously important that the children should be kept abreast of developing world affairs, though Jack's excitement had more to do with the simple fact of being able to listen for the first time to a proper radio. Till then at home they had only had crystal sets and earphones.

He spent a year at the school before returning for a final stint at St Philip's. No judgment appears to have been made on whether or not he was cured of whatever his illness was supposed to be. Perhaps a year was all that could be offered, given the demand for places when tuberculosis was still a much-feared killer.

It was at St Philip's, a small state school in a poor area, that Jack Trevor Story's writing talent was first noticed. His perceptive teacher was a Mr Covill, who covered a number of subjects but was a fervent admirer of the war poet Rupert Brooke. In those days it was possible to proclaim such an enthusiasm even in a place like Romsey Town (more evidence of the respect accorded to writers then). Jack was encouraged to concentrate on it, and promised that he (Mr Covill) would speak to the editor of the *Cambridge Daily News* about a job as a reporter, when he was ready to leave school.

Meanwhile he had begun to write in desultory fashion in his spare time. The family had moved on from Great Eastern Street (rent arrears was always a problem) and were inhabiting two rooms over a sweet shop in East Road. Across the street was a newsagent's, so that the progress of world events could be followed simply by looking out of the window and reading the latest billboard posters each morning. The rise and fall of the R101 airship and the flights of Jim Mollison and Amy Johnson were among the running stories that year. But one morning there appeared a poster advertising a new magazine called *Thriller*, and more interestingly, a competition with a £100 prize for a 30,000 word story suitable for publication in it. This was sufficient incentive for Jack to write 10,000 words in laborious longhand in a valiant attempt to win the prize. That was about as far as he managed to get before the competition closed, largely because his spare time was so much occupied with jobs and household chores. But it marked the beginning of serious literary endeavour. He read all the crime novels in the local library to try to learn how it was done, and with the same aim in mind copied out extracts from the writings of more classical authors with painful slowness. Another passion was aeroplanes (they could be seen from nearby Duxford performing amazing aerobatics almost over their heads in the school playground), so they naturally figured prominently in his early work. One story he particularly remembers was called "The Phantom Squadron". This tale harked back to the biplane battles of the First World War. The heroic squadron would suddenly appear out of the sun or clouds in moments of crisis to save the day, much like the US cavalry; but then when the danger had passed or the battle had been won, it would mysteriously vanish. Later, on the ground, questions would be asked about whom these brave aviators might be. Gradually it emerged that they couldn't be identified - and here the reader would experience a moment of *frisson*. Except that there were no readers, for this story, like many others, was immediately rejected.

There were no readers, that is to say, except for one: Jack's mother. Her own entrepreneurial energies had begun to flag and she was at this time working at the Chiver's jam factory, out of town at Histon. That was one reason why chores tended to fall on Jack, who was home from school before the others had returned from their various jobs (Elsa was evidently back with them by now). But Rhoda was ambitious for her children, and in Jack's case this even extended to re-writing his stories in her own faultless hand, for Jack's own handwriting seems at that stage to have been barely legible. Then they began to recognise the need for having the work typed. Neither of them could do this, so that meant a third stage, and one that had to be

paid for (albeit in pence rather than pounds) before the
manuscripts could be submitted to the magazines. They
suffered instant rejection, even so. Never once in this period
did the diligent young author receive so much as a word of
encouragement from the anonymous people running magazines
like *Modern Boy, The Magnet* and *The Gem.* Then, as ever,
breaking into print was a hard, hard business. What kept him
going was a simple desire for fame (prompted largely by the
movies), together with a feeling of being a professional rejected
writer, rather than simply a schoolboy, office boy or errand
boy like everyone else. (His mother may well have hoped that
money would actually be made, for with all the hardship her
health had begun to deteriorate and continuing to work at the
kinds of jobs that were open to her was becoming a great
strain.) Jack was further discouraged when the Regent School
of Journalism responded to a sample story by telling him that
his writing was so bad, they couldn't even accept him as a
student. *Thriller* magazine appeared in 1931. His first
accepted short story was published in *John O'London's Weekly*
in 1944.

Fortunately, writing was by no means Jack's only enthusiasm in
his early teenage years. He seems to have been into everything
just then: model-making, radios, aeroplanes, girls (of course),
music - all competing for his limited spare time. And there was
to be even less of that available once he had left school.

The year at the Open Air School had effectively spoiled his
chances of moving on into Secondary Education. He had a
sympathetic teacher, however, in Mr Covill, who did indeed as
promised talk to the editor of the *Cambridge Daily News*. He
also investigated the possibility of Jack's entering the Royal Air
Force. In both cases, rather predictably, he drew a blank. But
he explained in kindly fashion to the boy that the way forward
would lie in activities after he had left school - that would be
how he would gain the kind of education that was right for him.
Jack seems to have accepted the teacher's sincerity, and indeed

his words have turned out entirely true - most obviously in the case of Jack's writing, but also in the field of electronics, for he went on to attend night school in furtherance of an industrial career for no less than seven years. That is the hard road that people who miss out on higher education have to travel. Few have the stamina.

But all that was in the future; at the time of actually leaving school the prospects for getting on in the world did not look good, as the headmaster of St Philip's made all too clear when he addressed the leaving class. The school had a rather fine piano which was the pride and joy of the music teacher. To deliver his farewell speech, the headmaster, in heavy boots (evidently the standard adult footwear of the time), clambered insensitively onto its polished top, the better to command the attention of the rabble down at floor level. But the man was more than a little eccentric. He prefaced his remarks with a reference to something he had observed in the town the previous day:

"Yesterday, I saw two St Philip's boys walking through Petty Cury with their hands hanging by the sides of themselves, and the fingers extended. That is a form of *lunacy*! The fingers should be drawn up into a firm - but not tight - fist. That is the proper way for St Philip's boys to walk . . ." And here he demonstrated the correct technique by walking a few steps along the piano top. As to the world outside, into which they were now passing:

"You will be mixing with roadsweepers, dust-bin men, common labourers and the like, who will swear at you a good deal. Do not pay any attention. Remember that you are St Philip's boys - our *ambassadors* . . ." It didn't occur to the man that some at least might actually secure decent jobs for themselves. His allusions to lunacy were unfortunate, for only a few years later, when Jack was working at Pye Radio, in the Model Shop, he heard that the headmaster had been taken to Fulbourn mental home.

Aged fourteen, upon leaving school Jack immediately found *office* work, as a kind of odd-job boy with J O Vinter's, the coal merchants, seven-and-sixpence a week. His duties involved addressing mountains of buff envelopes, making tea for the men (in vile blackened tin mugs), operating a frightening paper press with whirling flywheels and swinging weights (without ever understanding what the machine actually did), nailing labels on coal wagons bound for such unexotic destinations as Wigan and Doncaster and generally making himself useful. As soon as he received his first week's pay, he hurried round on his bike to the home of a certain Mrs Fisk. Mrs Fisk was the only known guitar teacher in the neighbourhood.

Jack's interest in music had been much stimulated, as noted, by the seductive sounds emanating from the Premier dance hall back in Burwell. These were the early days of pop records, too - sixpence each from Woolworth's - so it was possible to listen to the hits of the day ("Jericho", "Valencia", "Baby Face" etc) at home. Then as now, a teenager would know all the current hits by heart. And after listening had come the thought of actually *making* music.

He had also discovered in the neighbourhood a tiny music shop owned by an old man who resembled the churchyard convict in David Lean's film of *Great Expectations*. Always sleeping in the window, on top of layers of sheet music, was a cat which spanned its full width. The proprietor was frightening in appearance but easy to talk to, if a little eager to force his own musical ideas on the customer. Jack first approached him with the thought of buying a second-hand guitar, or possibly a ukelele, but the old man had other advice.

"No, my boy, you don't want a guitar," he would say. "What you need is a *mandolin*. That is the most important instrument. The mandolin is the *leader* of the orchestra. Yes, the mandolin led the orchestra *long* before the violin. The violin is a *modern* instrument . . ." This became something of a ritual. He would then go on to show the boy his most prized possession - not a mandolin of impeccable pedigree, strange to say, but an ancient three-string double bass, with a lot of history attached to it. In the end Jack never did manage to buy what he wanted from the tiny shop, though money was doubtless a factor, too.

Meanwhile, his brother Pete had bought a guitar on weekly terms, and then either lost interest in it or failed to keep up the payments. At any rate, one way or another it fell into Jack's hands, and this was the instrument in his possession when he arrived at Mrs Fisk's door. The lady quickly sized him up - at fourteen, he was still wearing short pants - and explained sadly that she taught exclusively *classical* guitar. But the boy said that that would be quite all right (secretly not having the foggiest idea what she meant). Next she told him how much the lessons would cost: seven-and-sixpence a week. That was more crucial - his *entire* week's earnings! There would be nothing left to give his mum, never mind pocket money. Feeling glum, he rode slowly home and explained the situation to his mother. He expected to have to give up the idea, but to his surprise she urged him to go ahead with the lessons, promising to continue providing him with pocket money for the time being. Thus it was that this ambassador of St Philip's school in the slums of Romsey Town began receiving weekly tuition in classical guitar from a lady of education and refinement.

It didn't last long - the position in which he was expected to hold the instrument was beyond his strength for one thing - but from Mrs Fisk he did learn (amongst less relevant things) the simple fingering, scales and chords that constitute the basis of all guitar playing. Before very long he would set his brief classical training aside and join "Ron's Rebels", a semi-pro jazz band.

The coal merchants didn't pay enough, so he left in favour of an errand-boy job with a local butcher's, one of a chain of shops, at double his former wage. His work in the butchery trade - it lasted three years - has served Story well as a source of raw material for his short stories and journalism. Especially recommended reading is a *Guardian* piece, subsequently reprinted in *Letters to an Intimate Stranger*, entitled "The Good Dripping Guide".

It's likely, I suppose, that hardly anyone under forty now knows what dripping is. When I myself was a boy in the forties, every working-class household had a basin of the stuff in the pantry at all times. It was spread thickly on bread, like butter, then plenty of salt added. No doubt nowadays it would be regarded with disdain as having little nutritional value. Indeed, all the salt probably made it actually harmful. But there was nothing like bread and dripping for assuaging hunger during the austerity years after the war. A decade or two earlier, dripping had also been important in the early, hungry boyhood of Jack Trevor Story. At the bottom of the basin, invisible unless it was made of glass, there always resided the dark jelly - and here we differ in our remembered appreciation of what he has called "the golden essence of good living". For Jack, breaking through to the jelly was like a gluttonous orgasm; whereas for me it was a moment of horror.

Dripping, he maintains, is what kept the lower orders in happy subservience. "It came from fatted calves, from haunches, saddles and hindquarters. From great crackling roasts that only the wealthy can afford." The only reason the feudal system fell apart was that as the population grew there wasn't enough dripping to go round.

He once applied for a position as pantry boy at Lord Huntley's (of Huntley & Palmer's biscuits) large house in Peterborough, where he was shown Lord Huntley himself, then an old man, walking slowly round the garden. "Do you want to see him go round again?" the butler asked, having decided against the boy. "Or would you care for a slice of bread and dripping?" Thus was the harmony between gentry and peasantry maintained. "True socialists," Story writes, "don't hate or resent the rich, they *are* the rich, just as long as they're getting their dripping regularly."

Even so, the dripping he prepared as a butcher's boy for the passing tramp trade, tuppence a bag, must have been foul stuff - melted down from the stale, rotten, mildewy bits of fat, with even the scrunchy scraps fried down to a state of chemical inertness. "A crime against humanity," he calls it, though the manager of the shop explained to him that tramps died if they ate fresh food.

Despite the improvement in young Jack's pay, the wages for errand boys must indeed have been poor in relation to business profitability, for it was then economic to send them great distances with perhaps only a pound of sausages in the basket. But at least there was no temptation for the hungry boy to steal, as happened when carrying larger loads, especially if, as with pork pies, the item didn't require cooking. Pork pies were sold by the dozen, though always with the traditional thirteenth pie included. The innocent new boy would imagine that this extra pie was almost there for the taking, but people - customers and shopkeepers alike - had sharp eyes in those days.

"Fuck-pig," the manager said one day to his new employee. "I know you're eating the thirteenth pie. Don't let it happen again."

"No, Mr Harlow. I won't, Mr Harlow," replied the boy, sensing instantly that to deny the charge would be fruitless - and of course making no complaint about the extraordinary nickname. A shop manager could treat an errand boy exactly as he pleased then, especially if the boy hadn't got a father to come to his defence. But Jack found a way of compensating, at least for the loss of the occasional porkpie on his errands. (Beyond using an equally offensive name in reply, there was no answer to "Fuck-pig".)

The butcher also sold eggs. He used to go down to the mart in the city to bid for them, then send his hapless errand boy to bring back to the shop whatever bargain quantity he had purchased. In those days eggs were sold loose - not in today's handy cardboard packs - and the only container Jack had for carrying them was the basket on the front of his bike. Thus he would find himself faced with the task of transporting a huge quantity, in a great unstable pile, over the cobble stones back to the shop on Mill Road. The only consolation was that there were too many eggs to count (they would be sold by weight) so that breakages could be discarded, or left where they dropped, as the journey proceeded. And he could also eat them with impunity. Compared with the raw liver at the Open Air School, swallowing an egg straight from the shell was something to look forward to. The skilful young cyclist soon learned to crack the shell on the handlebar with one hand as he bumped along the busy roads, afterwards removing the evidence with the back of the same hand. Mr Harlow would never know.

The most dramatic incident in Story's youthful career in the butchery trade is told fairly factually in "Thursday Afternoon Early Closing", a short story sold (unusually) to one of the girlie magazines. None of the butcher's shops in the chain had their own refrigerator in those days; as meat began to go off it would be taken down to the brine vats in the cellar and afterwards sold as salt meat. Fresh joints and other still-valuable cuts, though, were transported by bike to the factory on East Road, where they were stored in a big, walk-in refrigerator. This was a job that fell to Jack on Saturday evenings (the shop having remained open until 8pm). On one occasion, instead of the usual Miss Nightingale being on hand to enter the refrigerator with him, he found himself teamed up with a new and rather lovely but unknown girl. They went inside in the normal way and were busy storing the meat Jack had brought when they heard the approaching whistle of a happy-go-lucky worker, who, in a single deft movement, banged the door down and continued on his whistling way.

Even today, Story admits to being a terrible coward. Once, not many years ago, he was sailing on the Thames with his friend Bill Johnson, and suddenly believed they were out of control and heading for the Teddington waterfall. He lost his voice from screaming so much, while a much-irritated Bill dealt single-handedly with the practicalities of the situation. So when the thick, soundproof refrigerator door banged shut and the light went out, young Jack went into a blind and terrified panic. Fortunately his companion, notwithstanding her good looks, was made of sterner and more resourceful stuff. First she touched him on the shoulder to calm him down; then she talked to him quietly, explaining how they were going to get out of their predicament.

"I'll take off my shoe and bang on the pipes with the heel," she said. "The pipes run all round the building and the sound will travel."

This she calmly did, while he stood helplessly by in the dark. Soon the door was lifted again, surprised faces appeared, and they were free. They hadn't even begun to shiver.

Jack Trevor Story has written that he went to *all* the Cambridge colleges as a young man - delivering sausages! But while he was still at school, back in the Great Eastern Street days before she moved on to the Chivers' jam factory, his mother had worked as a bed-maker, and in the kitchens, starting work at 5.30am. This brought the Storys their *first* contact with the great university that dominates the town. The university virtually fed the family then, for she was able to bring home bags of crusts that had been cut from the bread before it was served at table, along with other discarded but nutritious tit-bits. In his later years in broadcasting and the newspapers, sometimes meeting old Cambridge men, Story has been able to establish that his poor overworked mother, dragging herself home across Parker's Piece with her bag of crusts, would have passed the likes of Alistair Cooke and Gilbert Harding, out for a leisurely stroll. Although still only fifty, she suffered from a hernia (having to wear a crude iron truss), varicose veins, leg ulcers (great beetroot-like eruptions), piles and a permanent stomach complaint for which she constantly took indigestion powder, but which at the time of her death in 1957 was found to be a ruptured diaphragm. Sometimes upon reaching home she would faint away on the floor, whereupon the frightened children would have to rub her hands to revive her.

And she was a sensitive woman, too. One day Jack found the following note in a shoebox in which she kept important documents:

Notes on Myself

All my worry has brought me no sense of truth and less of reality. I wonder what one must experience to find that. In the self-pity that comes to me I seem incapable of being sure of anything except my own depression. The question arises - what can I do to escape from added suffering? To think, to feel, one must suffer. But I am unable to escape the thraldom of imaginative flights of fancy, and I am quite ashamed of my habit of day-dreaming and the strange and weird stories which I weave for myself. I look on it rather as a drug-taker may look on his drug - as something which is wrong but too pleasurable to be denied. But it is strange that I cannot put down in writing or express verbally those things which I see so clearly and so vividly in my mind.

I can see things happening. In my case, a struggle against overwhelming odds. In my mind I live it and identify myself with it. But like a musician without hands, I can find no medium of expression.

Another strange experience is that I suddenly realise at the age of 50, although my body has grown older my mind seems to have remained stationary, my intelligence and outlook that of a much younger woman. I cannot believe that youth has really passed.

I simply feel that I have passed through a deep experience which has brought me no happiness and from

which I have learned very little and that I have been
stunned, as though my experience of life has given me
concussion.

Now I will try to waste no more time on regrets.
Surely there is still some time left in which even I may
find some sort of reality.

Signed: R Story
(Wheatley, Malton)
August 1935

It's hard to believe that the author of this moving personal
statement also derived comfort from the poems of Patience
Strong, which she read over and over again, and that she
worried about the Royal Family, who she thought were not
really happy. Even with her many ailments, she didn't appear
morose. On the contrary, she was the one who always jollied
them along through all their troubles, laughing and singing
when she wasn't in actual physical pain. She seemed more
concerned about others than herself. (Elsa recalls that she used
to drop cigarette ends that she had specially collected at work in
a certain place where she knew tramps looked for them.)

Jack has written about all this in his autobiographical novel
Hitler Needs You (1970). His reaction on reading the secret
document was to make his mother a cup of tea, and then to try
to make himself receptive to whatever she might want to say.
But the tea was refused (as usual she had heartburn), and his
mother assumed from his behaviour that there must be
something wrong with *him*.

"How are your piles?" he asked finally. But she didn't want
to talk about them.

Descended as she perhaps was from the French aristocratic *De
Balles*, Rhoda Story did not feel rebellious towards the
prevailing social order. Despite the pain of her life, she

accepted - or at any rate did not question - the semi-feudal, town-and-gown system then operating so nakedly in Cambridge. Romsey Town was known as "Red Romsey" in some quarters, but there appears to have been little in the way of political organisation to justify that name. Those outside academic life were regarded - indeed referred to - as "servants". This applied to shopkeepers and other trade's people, as well as more direct employees of the university; and it was a fair description, for the uneducated people of the city were entirely dependent on it. To attack the university's privileges would have been - almost literally in many cases - to bite the hand that fed them.

Rhoda was only concerned that her children should learn from their betters, whether directly, or from what she herself had picked up. In spite of the menial labours she had to perform, she was rather a posh lady. When her eldest boy Ollie was on the boat to Australia, he wrote to tell her that he had met two engineers on board, who were nevertheless "all right". And he thought nothing of asking her to send him a book on etiquette. (He was already preparing himself for higher things, and would one day - curiously enough after a long period of living virtually as a tramp - manage an important radio station in New South Wales.)

So, in so far as any notion of class consciousness was being instilled into the children, they certainly weren't taught to feel solidarity with the lower orders, much as Rhoda was by nature a kindly woman. Their upbringing, Jack believes, was essentially classless, so that many years were to pass before any serious political opinions formed in his mind (though there *was* a brief, unthinking flirtation with the Mosleyites). He did not set out to become a writer in order to right the wrongs of the world, not even those committed against his mother.

In fact he had rather a good time in Cambridge, mingling and rubbing shoulders with the undergraduate classes. All the errand boys did. They copied the speech of their social superiors, and conversations between them, standing with their bikes on street corners, could sound to the casual listener as though they were being conducted in educated tones. Nor would the errand boys be mocking the undergraduates; the upper-class accents rubbed off on them without their realising it. Ever since, Jack Trevor Story's speech has contained odd phrases picked up then, such as "I say", and "ever so" (as in "It was ever so funny. . ."). This has done him no harm as a writer, but sometimes attracted comment during his years in industry.

Boating on the river was important for this social mixing of the local riff-raff with the sons of the upper classes, as also was music. Ron's Rebels were one of several semi-pro bands sought out for minor university engagements. In 1937 they won a *Melody Maker* dance-band competition, up against bands from all over the county. Jack himself took the prize for best guitarist. Music in those years was probably the most important of his many interests. After the *Melody_ Maker* publicity, he appeared at the Arts Theatre with the famous Quinca Gintas jazz band. Years later, his children were sceptical about the heights he claimed to have risen to in the thirties' music scene, until one day a girlfriend of one of his sons produced a rare photograph of the band, with Jack clearly recognisable amongst the musicians. It turned out that the girl's father had led the band in the same year. Jack Trevor Story's life has been full of coincidences of that sort.

After years of living in various unsatisfactory rooms - once they were left stranded with their possessions on the back of a coal cart when the promised new digs were found to be still occupied - the Storys at last got a brand new council house on Green End Road, in Chesterton. Elsa and Peter have remained in the area ever since. The move to the new house was very welcome for the family, but in Jack's mind it somehow marks the end of his best Cambridge days. He had put the butchery trade behind him, and had at last got a job at Pye Radio (close to home) after many rejected applications - first on a tedious assembly line, then in the Model Shop, where prototypes were built. He quickly developed a passion for research, and began attending night school, a time-consuming business.

During the brief assembly-line period at Pye, he had found himself looking at the back of the neck each day of a girl who performed the operation immediately prior to his. After work one evening he remarked to his mother, "I don't think the girl on the bench in front of me washes her neck."

If that were true, it only matched Jack's habitually grubby fingernails. He soon enough asked her out, and began courting her. And whatever the girl's faults, his mother, whose years in service had given her a sharp eye for minor social failings, seems to have been willing to overlook them, for she was accepted into the home readily enough. Indeed, the anxiety may have been the other way, for Elsa insists that Jack was nervous about introducing the girl to his family because of what *she* might think of *them*.

Evelyn Overton was his first proper date, his first girlfriend, and would be the first girl he made love to. Within a year or two she would become Jack Trevor Story's first wife.

Chapter Five

STORY'S WAR

Non, rien de rien, Non, je ne regrette rien . . . Everyone knows Edith Piaf's defiant, declamatory song, and applauds the sentiment behind it. It's a line taken by most famous or ambitious people - particularly those who flourish in the arts - when summing up their lives. Jack Trevor Story professes to be a soft, sentimental kind of man who cries easily, so you might expect him to be different. I was a little surprised, therefore, when the subject of regret came up in our conversations, to find him taking something close to the standard Edith Piaf line. There *was* an exception, however. He has been married twice (besides having had a family by someone he didn't marry, as will emerge later), and he regrets that on neither occasion was he in the least sensitive to the fact that a girl's wedding day is apt to be the most important day of her life. On the second occasion he was old and ill, and the marriage (to Elaine Hepple) was extraordinary in other ways; and at the time of his first marriage he was immature (aged just twenty) and under the familiar pressure. So he has his excuses. Even so, his insensitivity to his bride's feelings on these occasions is something he consciously regrets. Not many men of the arts would confess that much - or even *feel* regretful, their art being so much more important, for one thing.

Jack's foreman at Pye Radio was Ernie Triggs, a red-headed all-round musician and entertainer who tap-danced his way around the Model Shop in his white laboratory coat, improvising songs as he went:

> How'm I doin', hey, hey?
> Too too too too tow.
> Oh, how'm I doin', hey, hey?
> Gosh oh baby and how.

> Whatever I do be it understood,
> Whatever I do it's gotta be good, Story . . .

This performance would be interrupted by a sobering call from the office: "Mr Triggs. You're wanted . . ." The man was supposed to be working.

But when Jack approached this happy-go-lucky fellow for the time off to get married - on a Saturday morning - Ernie Triggs said, "So you're marrying little Evie, Story. All right, I'll give you half an hour."

It was raining on the day, and Jack rode to his wedding on his bike. In his pocket he had the latest edition of the *Melody Maker*, his bible then, published on Fridays. Waiting for him at the Registry Office were his mother, Evelyn herself, and the girl's father.

This man (her mother was dead and he had re-married, but the step-mother appears to have been absent from the ceremony) was a plumber by trade, though also, despite the handicap of a glass eye, a sculptor of some repute. He made gargoyles (replacement perhaps) for certain of the colleges, and more importantly was part-creator of the "Four Lamps", a piece of ornamental public sculpture that still stands at an intersection of footpaths in the middle of what used to be Parker's Piece. Extraordinarily, bearing in mind that Evelyn was of course pregnant, he had repeatedly warned Jack against marrying her on the grounds that she was quite incompetent at all the things a wife would be expected to do, such as cooking, housework - and indeed looking after a baby. "Run away from home!" he advised. "Go to sea! But don't *marry* her! She's still a *child*."

But fortunately for Evelyn and the baby, Jack, who did indeed have reservations about the marriage, had a stronger sense of responsibility. He had decided to ignore these exhortations from such an unlikely quarter and to go ahead with the ceremony. Marrying a girl you had got into trouble was very much the done thing in those days, and of course he did have some feeling for Evelyn - a pretty girl, blonde and petite - if he wasn't in love exactly. Sitting in the Registry Office waiting for the proceedings to begin and feeling less than intimately involved, he sought escape by burying his face in his *Melody Maker*, prompting the Registrar to exclaim:

"Mr Story, this *is* your wedding day!"

Afterwards Evelyn returned to the house on Green End Road, while Jack cycled thoughtfully back to the radio factory. It was still raining, even though the month was May (1937).

On the face of it, Jack and Evelyn were incompatible from the beginning. She is remembered (she died in 1978) as having been placid and undemanding, and at the same time rather coldly undemonstrative - qualities that don't always go together. Opinions differ as to whether she was truly, as a young wife and mother, the child-like creature her father judged her to be. (Philip Larkin has a well-known poem beginning, "They fuck you up, your mum and dad." It looks as though Evelyn's dad was having a fair shot at the job single-handed.) As might be expected, his opinion is fiercely contested amongst her own children. Her eldest daughter (that first baby) Jacqueline accounts for Evelyn's early ineptitude in domestic skills by pointing out what she really lacked was a decent role model. Her step-mother, a strict woman, was apparently too distant from her emotionally to fulfil that need. She is also seen as having by necessity become the rock of the growing family as Jack became less available as a husband and father, and less reliable as a provider. Perhaps *he* was really the childlike one. Knowing him today, one sometimes has the suspicion that he is a man who has never really grown up.

But certainly in the early days Evelyn does appear to have stood somewhat in Jack's shadow. And yet, if they were in some respects an ill-matched couple; they do seem to have had a certain *rhythmic* compatibility. They had a shared interest in dance music, and in fact their first date was at a dance. It was an afternoon affair at the Corn Exchange in Cambridge, where an Ideal Homes Exhibition was also being held. The band singer sang through a megaphone, and Jack still remembers one of the songs: "I'm Full of Vitamin A". Besides conventional dancing, they also roller skated to music, very popular just then. Jack has pleasant memories of surrendering to the rhythm and gliding easily round the floor with Evelyn on his arm, enjoying equally the music and the movement. It made a nice contrast with his more cerebral, sedentary activities. She also, as an early "groupie", followed his own dance-band playing - Ron's Rebels and the Pye band, Percey Cowel at the Dorothy Ballroom, in the open air on Christ's Piece one evening a week (no guitar amplification - just part of the rhythm), and in the band coach to Bedford for the police ball, Reg Cottage and his music - and all her life would sing by heart the old pop songs of the pre-war years. Although she would be supplanted in Jack's life by other women in other ways (though never as the mother of his first five children), Evelyn remained the closest to him musically. All of his women liked to sing in their various ways; but just as Burwell was Jack's special boyhood place, so the music of the twenties and thirties was - and remains - his special music, and that was Evelyn's province.

The first years of their married life were as conventional a domestic period as he would ever know. Of course, his private hobbies and activities didn't end with his marriage; but at the same time he was now taking his job pretty seriously, and he even took to growing vegetables - very competently, by all accounts - in his back garden. When the baby came along he had a special little seat made to attach to the crossbar of his bike, and took her for rides just like any other proud young dad.

But Jack had a roving eye, and far from putting her foot down, Evelyn, as time went by, would make it very easy for him to cultivate relationships with other women. Did he have a dominating personality then, at a time when men were far more in command of their domestic affairs than they are today? Was she afraid of him? Or did she perhaps have her own private reasons for putting up with his womanising? It's impossible to tell. And in fact these other relationships - often simply romantic, unconsummated (one might even say adolescent) attachments - would not pose much of a threat to their life together for some years. But then the role model she had always lacked would come into Evelyn's life in a most astonishing way. Meanwhile, though, there were the important war years to be lived through.

Those years begin in Story's memory on a winter's night in Cambridge, some time before war was actually declared, although everybody by then knew it was coming. He was playing in a trio at the University Arts Hotel and had to step outside because of an asthma attack. It was foggy outdoors, but the fog didn't seem to affect him. The street was deserted, but then he heard approaching foot-steps, and out of the gloom appeared a little man carrying a suitcase.

"Mr Simpson," said Jack, as he recognised the face (something he has never been good at).

"Hello, Story," the man replied, in a Geordie accent which confirmed his identity. "What are you doing here?"

Jack explained that he was playing in the band. He knew Mr Simpson from Pye's, where he had been a toolmaker. He had only recently left the company. "Where are you working now?"

"At Murphy's - Welwyn Garden City. Murphy Radio."

"What are you doing there, then?"

"I'm a foreman . . . Do you want a job?"

"Yes," said Jack eagerly, although he had not until that moment thought of leaving Pye.

"Are you skilled or semi-skilled?"

"Semi-skilled."

"It'll be two pounds ten shillings a week. Come and see me - any time. There'll be plenty of overtime, too. There's a war coming, you know." This was a big improvement on his present wage (wages do seem to have been curiously variable in those days), but Jack didn't immediately act on the offer. But then when the summer came around he and Evelyn and the baby were invited to spend a week at his Uncle Charlie's farm at Hertford (the same farm he had visited as a boy in search of his native air). One day he asked Uncle Charlie where Welwyn Garden City was and was surprised to learn that it was within cycling distance. He borrowed a bike, saw Mr Simpson, and got a job at Murphy's as promised, on the improved wage.

This was the first of a chain of events that would ultimately keep Jack Trevor Story out of the forces. Not that there was any particular calculation on his part. His father's brutal death in the First World War seems to have had a less than profound effect on his own attitude to war. As noted, he flirted with the British Union of Fascists in the late thirties. He admired Mosley, and even took their magazine, *Action*. This seems terrible now, but Story had no idea of what was happening to the Jews in Germany. He was simply giving rather lukewarm support to what seemed in his innocent brain a worthwhile cause. He may well, as the war approached, have been in some confusion as to what cause precisely he would be fighting for if he should have to go to war, but he had no real plan for evading enlistment.

As for Mr Simpson, he was a man who would continue to bob up unexpectedly in Story's life. Much later, visiting his sister Elsa in Chesterton one day he said, "Who's that man digging the garden over there?"

"Why, that's Mr Simpson," Elsa replied.

"That man is in my life!" exclaimed Jack.

"His son was going to marry one of your daughters - did you know that?"

Jack didn't know. By then he had too many daughters to keep track of. He remembers in particular gazing upon a beautiful set of toolmaker's squares, lying in a special baize-lined case, that Mr Simpson had made by hand, entirely without recourse to measuring instruments of any kind. They were accurate to one ten-thousandth of an inch. Story's preference is for a throw-away, undisciplined technique in his own profession, but this does not prevent him from admiring exquisite, painstaking craftsmanship of that kind. Indeed, he admires fine professional accomplishment in any field.

Jack Trevor Story's life has been a life of lateness. (He wasn't actually late for his wedding, though he *was* the last to arrive, as the perceptive reader may have noticed.) The habit no doubt derives from a dislike of timetables - of being ruled by the clock. (William Saroyan had the same problem: he once declined to keep an appointment with James Joyce in Paris on the ground that it was like being asked to breathe next Tuesday.) Story's daughter Jenny, commenting on the fact that he seldom takes a holiday abroad even when he can afford to, says that it's because he would expect the aeroplane to be ready to take off when *he* was ready. When he abandoned his career in electronics in the early fifties to become a full-time writer, the company magazine commented that he would chiefly be remembered for his lateness. When he gives talks to literary circles or takes creative-writing classes, his lateness is the most frequent complaint against him. In the fifties he was even late for a Royal Premiere, though he had the excuse that he had to deliver a dozen eggs and some money to Evelyn (whom he had by then left) on the way. Bill Johnson was the exasperated driver.

And this habit of lateness, Story insists, was the chief reason why he didn't go to war. When the time came, all eligible young men were required to present themselves on the appropriate day - it was done alphabetically - to sign on for war service. Jack's day duly arrived, but of course he got there breathlessly at the last minute, just as the door was closing. The bureaucracy was inflexible. There would be no point in coming back next morning, he was told, because tomorrow was for the 'T's, of which there were sure to be a great many, given the commonness of such names as Thompson, Thomas and

Taylor. And that was that. Latecomers could not be accommodated.

Story maintains that no further attempt was ever made by those officiating to rope him in; but Fate wasn't satisfied with this piece of bureaucratic good-fortune and was working on the problem of how to keep Jack Trevor Story out of the conflict from another angle, just to be sure. Waiting at Murphy Radio was the man who would steer him into the safe haven of a reserved occupation.

The man's name was W B Bartley. Story wrote a piece about him in *Punch* in 1987, the year after he died. It's a generous piece, and Story had good reason to write in that vein for there seems to have been little or no reason why Bartley should have chosen to treat him so well at such a crucial time. Bartley was the Chief Engineer. "He took a liking to me the way an engine driver takes to liking a good bit of rag," Story writes. But the fact was that he was immediately made an Approved Admiralty Inspector, despite a distinct lack of qualifications and experience (not to mention an unsuitable temperament).

Soon after the declaration of war a new law was enacted, forbidding people to change jobs. Bartley had meanwhile decided to move to Marconi's. He offered to take Jack with him, along with Mr Simpson and one or two other favoured underlings. They had to move fast to beat the law, though obstacles of that kind didn't appear to trouble Bartley. Soon they were all safely under his wing and command at the Marconi factory in St Albans. Marconi's were heavily engaged in important war work (or at least that was the general assumption).

Back at Pye's, Jack's foreman Ernie Triggs had been an eccentric. Mr Simpson, too, used to stand on his head in the middle of the shop floor, and had once been an all-in wrestler in America. W B Bartley rather surpassed these two, however. He had a voice like a sealion and never talked to anyone except in the way sealions talk to onlookers. A big, gingery man with a moustache - he resembled the comedian Harry Tate in both appearance and speech - he never wore socks, regardless of the company he was keeping. He hated to break off work - or more accurately talking about work - even for a moment, and when in conference in the boardroom, so as not to let the conversation die, would pee in the executive toilet with the door open and standing well back, so that he was at least half visible to everyone, his secretary included. He couldn't bear to see anyone sitting down on the job, even if the job consisted of watching some monotonous early experiment in automation. Several times Jack had his chair kicked from under him for this misdemeanour. When he protested, W B Bartley would bark, "I didn't sit down all the time I was a boy!" Impatient with any estimate, no matter how reasonable, of how long a job was going to take, he would cry, "Three dayeeeeees!" his voice rising like a siren on the last syllable. It was an expression much imitated around the factory.

Story writes that Bartley put him in charge of his hobbies. These were in fact special products aimed at post-war market opportunities - nothing to do with the war effort as such, except that they may have benefited from government contract funding. Story did hardly any war work at all during the war. At an early stage he was involved with exhaust testers for Russia. Evidently the Russians changed sides twice while the job was proceeding through the shop.   He also worked on bomb-release mechanisms, though that he believes was probably at Murphy's. Otherwise at Marconi's he was engaged in pH measurement and control in industrial processes, and in the development of specialised medical equipment. For a time he was quite probably the leading expert in the pH field in the whole of the country. The work took him into such diverse places as the London sewers, Battersea Power Station and the Bird's Eye custard factory. On the medical side he worked on a new audiometer connected with the development of hearing aids, and on an electro-encephalograph machine which measured brain rhythms and detected tumours and epilepsy. It has long puzzled him that the scientists were only concerned with a limited part of the brain's electrical activity - alpha and beta rhythms - and had no curiosity about wavelengths and frequencies outside their immediate scope. Ever since he has had the feeling that brain activity has never been fully explored, making him less of a sceptic on such topics as extra-sensory perception and spiritualism than he might otherwise have been.

He makes light of his own technical contribution, portraying himself as the intrepid labourer, at the command of men who far surpassed him in intelligence and knowledge. Yet surprisingly, decades later, he is still able to talk about electronics and instrumentation in convincing detail, when one might have expected such knowledge quickly to have evaporated once he began to apply himself full time to fiction writing. He occasionally brings this knowledge into his fiction, most notably in one of his more ambitious (not to say mystifying) novels of the seventies, *Morag's Flying Fortress*.

But whatever competence Story may have developed under his tutelage, Bartley seems always to have regarded him as an oddity. Once they were on a train, returning from a Manchester oil refinerary with Brockelsby, the Chief Physicist. The two had a habit of talking to one another over Story's head, ignoring the fact that he was actually present. Suddenly Bartley noticed him and reached across to hold his head, as though it were an inanimate object.

"You see, Brockelsby," he said. "Look at his bone structure."

Brockelsby looked and nodded, and they continued with their private discussion. Ever since, Story has felt that in that obscure incident he missed a vital clue to the secret of his real place on this planet.

At Marconi's, the war years merged into the post-war period without much of a step change so far as Jack was concerned. It is specifically the war years, however, that he remembers and describes as having been above all boring. He knows that life then was anything but boring for those fighting in the front line, or manning the warplanes, or dying in concentration camps; but for reserved occupationists it was a long war that seemed to last for years and years. Although the social pressure to enlist was far weaker than it had been for his father in the First World War, it seems likely that this apparent boredom was in reality an impatience for the war to end, for with London under bombardment it cannot have been altogether comfortable to be in one's twenties and still wearing civilian clothes. Certainly young Story wasn't inactive. Besides work, he had an increasingly difficult domestic life to contend with. They were now living in a council house in Welwyn Garden City. More children were arriving - after Jacqueline (1937) came Christine (1940) and Peter (1944) - but Evelyn appears to have remained somewhat at the novice stage as a mother and housekeeper, so that such routine tasks as washing the mountains of dirty nappies often fell to Jack. This would have absorbed most of the energies of any normal man, but he was living a full social life outside the house, too. Philanderers of necessity have to be pretty quick about their business as a rule; but Jack's technique with the girls he knew in those years was to court them romantically for months on end, taking them to the pictures, horse riding, and generally leading up very slowly to the final seduction, which in fact rarely occurred at all. One girlfriend, impatient with this diffident approach - he claimed to be afraid of her because she was too posh - suggested they go potato-picking together and sleep rough in a hut, then it might be all right. When he wasn't courting he had home-guard or fire-warden duties to perform. Disappointingly, he remembers little of this, except for all the terrible drilling, for which he was "excused boots" (like Alfie Bass in *The Army Game*) on account of his awful feet - all bunions and corns, inherited from his mother (who in her poorest and hardest-working days suffered agonies in second-hand shoes, in addition to her many other ailments). He somehow found the time to get involved in local amateur dramatics. And on top of everything else he was writing in every spare minute, still striving for that elusive breakthrough into print.

Marconi's seems to have been a hot-bed of literary ambition at that particular time. Amongst the young hopefuls, forever sending out short stories or radio scripts and having them returned instantly with the usual regretful rejection slip attached, was Ronnie Wolfe, who would one day rise to become a top television comedy writer. Jack and Ronnie were different writers, different personalities. Jack was probably the more serious, but Ronnie was a more practical student of the literary scene and far more knowledgeable about such matters as who were the best writers to read and what was being published. Story hardly ever read or even thought about, other writers; he was too busy. Eventually, though, Ronnie Wolfe persuaded him to read a few writers who might conceivably be useful to him. One such was Gerald Kersh. Jack read him, without any noticeable effect. Next (the year was 1944) Ronnie said, "Try William Saroyan."

"Who?"

"William Saroyan. There's a new collection of stories just out - *Dear Baby*. Buy it! Get someone to buy it for you if you can't afford it!"

Jack's girlfriends tended to be well-to-do, and were inclined to indulge him. The current one was Betty Kembrey, a radio operator. He had only to mention the book for her to buy him a copy - a slim, plain volume, printed in accordance with war-time regulations. That evening he sat down and read it. The book changed his life.

Nowadays William Saroyan, in Britain at any rate, is a considerably more elusive author than Jack Trevor Story. You won't find *any* of his books in the libraries or bookshops. In 1944, however, the position was very different. Saroyan was close to being as famous and influential as Hemingway then. He had won the Pulitzer Prize for his play *The Time of Your*

Life, had published a number of highly successful volumes of short stories, and had recently had a big bestseller with his first novel *The Human Comedy* (successfully filmed, starring Mickey Rooney). He was a writer strongly in the American unschooled tradition, the model for every semi-educated young man with a typewriter and a burning belief that he had something to say. All over the world they were pounding out their novels and short stories much as Jack was doing, largely inspired by Saroyan's earliest and most vital collection, *The Daring Young Man on the Flying Trapeze*, published in 1934. But Jack was altogether unaware that Saroyan was such an important writer. Nor did he appeal to him for the usual reasons. *Dear Baby* was a book written by a wealthy and world-famous author - now a private in the American army who with official permission was at that very moment occupying an expensive room at the Savoy Hotel in London, writing a novel to promote Anglo-American relations - not a raw collection of autobiographical stories revolving around an unknown and poverty-stricken young writer desperately trying to preserve his integrity in the midst of the Great Depression. But Saroyan was still Saroyan in spite of all the success he was enjoying. The title story of the 1944 collection is a heartbreaking tale about a boxer coming up to a championship fight whose wife has just died in childbirth. Jack cried over the story. It was the first time he had been deeply moved by someone else's writing.

But Saroyan's impact on him wasn't simply emotional; *Dear Baby* had other messages, too. Till then his writing had been largely imitative and full of clichés. Aspiring writers (British ones at any rate) tend to feel encouraged when they reach the stage of being able to string clichés together without too much effort. This facility can be mistaken for a real ability to write, when in fact it is simply an imitation of educated middle-class language - the old BBC standard English. Evelyn's father had been telling Jack over and over again that he would never become a writer, because you had to go to college for that. He had the common belief that there is a standard, correct way of writing, and that the student's task is simply to master this. That was what Jack had been trying unconsciously to do. Saroyan's first lesson was how to be yourself in your writing - how to get your faults and limitations onto paper *intact*, not to strive to correct them. That was the only route to an original voice, without which no writer basically in the business of selling his personality rather than imparting information could hope to gain an audience.

Saroyan also taught him that there was no need to be over-concerned about plot, or characterisation. The events of real life never unfolded in the way that the plot of an O'Henry story unfolds, and it was more important to try to impart a real feeling for life than to construct an artificial tale with a surprise ending. Similarly, fictional characters need not be exaggerated versions of the real thing, always speaking their favourite lines on cue, like Mr Micawber in Dickens, or for that matter Mrs Mop in the radio comedy of the war years, *Itma*. It wasn't necessary to do more than observe people in ordinary life; and moreover, to look for their common humanity beneath the surface instead of dwelling on the superficial characteristics that seemingly made them so very different from one another.

Dear Baby can be read in a single sitting. Jack laid the book aside after finishing the last story and went to his typewriter as a new man. This time he began to write a short story without worrying about trying to achieve an educated tone. He used the kind of words he preferred to use himself, rather than the longer and more pompous sort he had groped for hitherto. The title he gave this new story was "Peter Keeps a Secret". It was about a young man who died before his time and arrived in Heaven to find the authorities there strangely unprepared to receive him. Indeed, equipping him with his own personalised wings and harp and the rest of the paraphernalia required for eternal life proved so difficult and disruptive that they elected to send him back.

The tale was nothing like any of the stories in *Dear Baby*, proving that he really had understood the message. Instead, it was unmistakably a Jack Trevor Story tale.

He showed the result of this inspired performance to Ronnie Wolfe, who asked where he intended sending it.

"Oh, to *Woman's Own*, perhaps. One of the usual magazines, you know . . ."

"Don't send it there! You're literary, Jack. Send it to a *literary* magazine."

"Like what?"

"*John O'London's Weekly*. Try them."

Jack duly posted off the manuscript, enclosing the usual stamped envelope for its expected return. Instead he got a personal letter from the editor, Wilson Midgeley (he introduced crossword puzzles into this country), in his blue fountain pen. "I like this very much," Midgeley said. Also enclosed was a cheque for six guineas.

Story's war was above all non-hazardous. He makes little attempt to conceal this, feeling, one imagines, that his father's death in the earlier war was sufficient patriotic sacrifice for several generations of the family. Living and working in and around London, he was of course exposed to the same hazards as any civilian; but the bombs fell on others. He got used the sight of heaps of rubble where homes had once stood, and learned to go about his business. There was no alternative. He even took Evelyn and the kids for trips out in a little Austin Seven he had bought when he had a job to do away from the factory - late in the war, when the V1 flying bombs were making life in the capital very uncomfortable once more. One day he left the family in the car while he went into a factory to perform some task or other connected with instrumentation he had installed. He was perched on top of a vat, fiddling with the equipment, when there was a sudden explosion and he fell several feet to the ground. He had suffered nothing more than a little bruising, however, and so resumed his work, totally forgetting about Evelyn and the children, outside in the street. Returning to the car later, he said:

"Did you hear that explosion?"

"That wasn't an explosion - that was a *bomb!*" said Evelyn indignantly. "You might have come out!" But she was a stoical lady who was soon feeding bits of sandwich to Christine, saying, "Eat up, eat up . . ." Jack used to imagine these trips were pleasurable outings for her.

One evening in the summer of 1945 he met his radio operator girlfriend Betty Kembrey as usual to go to the pictures. She was flustered. A momentous message had come through to the effect that hostilities had ceased. She had tried to convey this to Churchill, whose staff couldn't immediately locate him.

"You know the war's over before he does," she said to Jack.

Chapter Six

PROFESSIONAL WRITER

Jack Trevor Story has always found it difficult to let his women go. Many relationships have been life long - in his head if not in actuality. In the case of Betty Kembrey, this determined attachment had begun at the moment of first meeting. It was at a Marconi's Christmas party, during the war. They were for some reason obliged to shake hands, and Jack, having taken an instant fancy to her, used the trick of pretending to have forgotten to let go. Their real relationship lasted for three years - until the victory celebrations of 1945, after which she had to return to her home and post office job in Swansea. Jack was heart-broken. Their love had been something special. They hadn't made actual love, but that was evidence of the strength of his feelings for the girl. Always, he says, in his younger adult life at any rate, true love caused that incapacity. Betty in fact seems to have been extraordinarily innocent, for she once believed that she might become pregnant simply because he had sat on the edge of her bed (in her lodgings) when she was ill. The pain of parting was felt with equal intensity on both sides. He remembers passing the house she had lived in one evening and kissing the gatepost. Some months after leaving she arrived back at the factory gates, unannounced, to ask if he wanted to marry her. He took her out to a local cafe for a meal, but now something had happened and he had to make it clear that there was another obstacle to their marrying besides the obvious one of his wife and kids. While she had been away, he had met, and more importantly bedded, a secretary at Marconi's, Ross Woods. The new development in his life could be conveyed without his being explicit because it conformed with a firm prediction Betty had made before their first parting. She had said he would make love to the first woman who came along, that she would be in his life for twenty years, and would ruin it. Now the first part at least had happened, and Betty picked up the message that there was no future for her in the relationship. She returned home tearfully to Wales a second time. Jack never saw her again, though she has remained strongly in his heart and mind ever since.

Ross Woods was another of Marconi's ambitious writers. Her forté - in fact her obsession - was western novels. Jack describes her as "totally a cowboy". Allowing for the normal exaggeration or caricature in his thumb-nail sketches of the people in his life, it does appear to be the case that in those days she wore cowboy clothes in the full sense. She worked in the administration building (a converted country house), some distance from the factory, which she rarely had reason to visit. In spite of this inconvenience, at a time of strong need in her life, she took a fancy to Jack and began to plan how she might snare him. A useful go-between was another spare-time scribbler by the name of Frank Lloyd. Frank was unpublished and looked up to Jack, who had of course by now broken into print. The way that Jack himself tells the tale is that Frank Lloyd had a mission to bring the two literary soul-mates together in the teeth of strong disinterest on both sides. He somehow persuaded them to join him for lunch, after a small football pools' win. The date was not a success, for Jack has always hated the idea of lunch, a ritual cherished by many conventional people. Undeterred, Frank next persuaded him to join Ross in a baby-sitting evening at his house. Once again both were supposedly reluctant, but they nevertheless complied. That, as I say, is Jack's version; but there is surely clear evidence of a hidden hand at work here - the hand of Ross. She turned up for the baby-sitting date looking like Marlene Dietrich in *Destry Rides Again*. Jack's lustful passions, if not his finer feelings, were aroused. Soon he was visiting her at her home in Bricket Wood, when her husband was out working in the evenings (roping in barrage balloons, or something of that sort). After the long, chaste affair with Betty Kembrey, here was a girl outside his marriage that he could actually do it with. It was his first successful excursion into real adultery. As for Ross, a sexually disastrous ten-year marriage had left her still a virgin, so she was a more than eager participant. One evening her husband returned from his balloons with a witness and caught the two almost in the act. A bizarre touch was that Jack had with him Christmas presents for his children.

"So this is what you get up to behind my back!" the man exclaimed - always a weak line from deceived husbands. Ross's response was to walk out and move into a flat across the green from Jack's marital home, on Meadway in Welwyn Garden City.

"I didn't love Evelyn, you know," Jack will say today. Or, "I never loved Ross. Never." And yet - to take Evelyn first - he admits that it took him an awfully long time to have complete sex with her. He would only make the attempt in circumstances where he could feel emotionally secure, such as behind the gasworks, or in someone else's house when they were baby-sitting. One might surmise, therefore, that he had stronger romantic feelings for Evelyn when they were both young than he now remembers. (A girl named Vera Root was supposedly the great love of his adolescent years, though he scarcely managed ever to speak to her.) The suggestion certainly causes him to ponder. Usually he is very impatient with deductive reasoning, or jumping to obvious conclusions. Once he was sent home from Pye Radio, with loss of pay, for holding Evelyn's hand (it seems he has always been a great hand-holder), so there must have been some tenderness in their early relationship. It is hard to judge how she looked then because there are no surviving photographs. She hated to pose to have her picture taken and wouldn't have kept the snaps anyway as she couldn't bear - so her daughters say - to look back.

Ross, Jack says, knew from the beginning that he didn't love her romantically. She was desperate to escape from a loveless marriage, and also very much wanted children. The young engineer in the laboratory (she used to leave him gifts of fruit) happened to be the man she fell for when these feelings were strong. He was available at least on a part-time basis, and susceptible to manipulation. Yet there must have been something strong and genuine between them. This, after all, was the young woman who as much as Evelyn and the kids stood in the path of marriage to his beloved Betty Kembrey. Once he had slept with Ross he was committed to her, he says, but that obviously hasn't been true of all his girlfriends. Why was Ross different? At the very least they were enthusiastic lovers in those early days, if a passage in Jack's memoir *Dwarf Goes to Oxford* is to be believed. Once they climbed the iron spiked fence around St Albans cemetery and made love on top of a stone mausoleum whilst waiting for buses to take them in different directions to their respective homes and spouses. Nor was the dark necessary. On another occasion they had sex on top of a tarpaulined strawstack close to the Marconi factory, in the hot sunlight. And there were similar adventures with Ross, during that long hot summer of 1947, in Welwyn Woods, where *The Trouble with Harry* was conceived. For a romantic through and through (his own description), who sees himself as one of the very few male writers who writes about love, and who despises the macho-strut of novelists like Hemingway, Jack Trevor Story seems excessively fond of using the word *fuck* when talking about these intimate encounters with some of the women of his life. He uses it pretty liberally where Ross is concerned. She was doubtless too easy, and it is well known that men have a tendency to take advantage of women like that, only to disparage them in crude terms later. One must conclude either that he wanted to diminish her emotional importance in his past life, or that he finds euphemisms more objectionable than plain language. Maybe both.

But whatever the truth was about their relationship, Ross Woods was determined to have him even if he had to be shared with a wife and (in all likelihood) other girlfriends, and she had also to bear the disapproval of her own family. Once settled in the little flat (over shops) near Meadway, she was soon receiving Jack as a frequent visitor from across the green. His sister Elsa remembers him abruptly leaving a Christmas party, after being told there was somebody loitering at the gatepost. An attempt was made at first to keep the affair secret from Evelyn and the kids, but it was difficult to avoid meeting in the street and eventually he introduced her to the eldest of the children. "This is my girlfriend," he told them jokily, thereby skilfully giving the impression that the relationship was in fact innocent, without lying. The neighbourly affair continued, with Evelyn becoming suspicious but making no move; then Ross at that point seems to have hit accommodation trouble. A caravan from her mother's house at Bricket Wood, that would wind up parked on the Story's front garden, played some part in the emergency response to her sudden homelessness, but that sort of arrangement was evidently beneath her dignity. Jack thus appeared to be faced with the familiar choice of either leaving his wife to live with his girlfriend, or losing her. Any other man would in the end have made one choice or the other, but the ingenious inventor of short-story plots hit upon a third solution - one that most readers of *fiction* might well dismiss as incredible. He invited Ross to join the household. And so compelling were her various needs that she agreed.

This surely was the moment when Evelyn would at last take a stand and fight for her position as Jack's wife and the mother of his children - but no. And even more amazing, no sooner had Ross settled in than the two women became firm friends - "got on like a house on fire" is the phrase everyone uses - for they discovered that they had a powerful common interest and source of grievance, namely Jack Trevor Story. Evelyn may well have seen that Ross's position was in truth no more secure or happy than her own. Jack, she knew, would not be any more content with two women at home than he had been with a single wife. Before long, in all probability - if not already, in fact - he would be seeking sexual gratification (or romantic friendship) elsewhere, leaving his two domestic women to manage a home that had always proved too much for one.

And sure enough Ross, a lady of tidy and methodical habits, soon began to put her own stamp of efficiency and order on the running of the large household on Meadway. This was very welcome for Evelyn, who in addition to a stubborn incompetence in these things also suffered from terrible phobias, which made it next to impossible for her to cope with dirty nappies and the vomit of sick children. Now she had a friend and ally who could deal with those things with a shrug of the shoulders, which meant that it would no longer be necessary to send in desperation for a neighbour whenever domestic emergencies arose. She hated cooking, too, while Ross rather enjoyed it. All this pointed to an obvious solution: Ross should be the one to stay at home and look after the house, whilst Evelyn, to her great relief, would go to work again.

The children were soon calling this new lady in their lives "Aunty Ross" (one presumes that she had by now toned down the cowboy attire). Her presence in their midst did not seem particularly strange for the simple reason that no-one explained to them that this was a highly unconventional, not to say immoral domestic arrangement. Children accept whatever comes along, provided it doesn't hurt or frighten them. Ross, like Evelyn - this was one of the few things they had in common - was emotionally undemonstrative and not given to cuddling people, whether children or adults. But she was a kindly lady for all that, who could often leave the kids little presents by their bedsides for them to wake up to. (Her housekeeping competence was a revelation to Evelyn. Later, when she had to cope once more unaided, she would begin to put to work the methods she had learned from Ross - the only useful role model she had ever had.) The happy two-mum arrangement might have continued longer had not Ross herself been pregnant the whole time.

Pushed somewhat to the sidelines of his own domestic life in this period, and past the age thirty now, Jack the writer was straining to build on the solitary short story that Wilson Midgeley had published in *John O'London's Weekly.* His capacity for work and invention was astonishing, bearing in mind that he was still doing a demanding full-time job in engineering. Jacqueline can remember the sound of his typewriter late into the night. Then, as later - and in fact down to the present day - he could manage with a minimal amount of sleep. Similarly, he could absorb a heavy load of rejection. Fifty-eight more stories (it's a figure he has repeated many times in print and interviews and was probably accurate) went out - mainly to *John O'London's* - and came back again without comment. He tried other magazines, too, notable *Argosy,* after a long period of being put off by its claim to publish only the very best in contemporary fiction; and it was *Argosy* he believes, which finally accepted something to break this long run of short-story rejections. These literary magazines didn't pay much, though. For proper reward he had to wait until 1949, and his first *John Bull* acceptance. They could afford to pay fifty pounds, a tidy sum in those days. "New to the Job", which appeared in the September 17 issue, was illustrated by Ronald Searle, then relatively unknown. The story reflected Jack's industrial background - a new employee on a production line in a radio factory gradually becomes aware of the rotting dreams of his fellow workers, chained by mundane needs to the factory bench. The appearance of his name in such a well known magazine might have seemed like fame at last; but Story was soon to discover that the names of short-story contributors to newspapers and magazines were in the main no better known to the general public than those of hack journalists.

But more exciting even than a story in *John Bull* was the fact that a novel had recently been accepted, *Green to Pagan Street.* Most Jack Trevor Story fans assume that his first acceptance was *The Trouble with Harry,* but this very different early novel had that distinction. *Green to Pagan Street* (a misleading title, perhaps, in as much as "green" refers to traffic lights, and "Pagan" appears to have no special significance) bore William Saroyan's influence, as was noticed by the *Sunday Times'* reviewer. It is the simple story of life in a slum street facing demolition, and of an ambitious boy who dreams of fame as a writer and romance with the daughter of an Italian cafe owner. The book wasn't actually published until 1952 (hence the confusion), by which time much else had happened.

In fact Story's writing career had begun to develop along very different lines from *Green to Pagan Street*. By the late forties he had discovered that he possessed a remarkable facility for writing short comedy thrillers. Already a fair number (he talks about more than a hundred, but that surely cannot be true) had begun to accumulate - post rejection - in his tea chest. They would come in very useful in a few years time, but for the present they seemed like so much waste paper. One was very special, however. When he was writing the story he had the title, "Where Town and Country Meet" (a big roadside sign as you entered Welwyn). Then he saw a Saroyan title (a collection of stories published a decade earlier), *The Trouble with Tigers,* and re-named his own short book *The Trouble with Harry*. Searching through the reference books he had found an American publishers with offices in London who might be more suitable for his new style of writing, T V Boardman. They accepted *The Trouble with Harry* and published it in 1949. Macmillan brought it out in America, and soon this tale of the misadventures of a corpse in a wood would catch the macabre attention of the great film producer Alfred Hitchcock.

Meanwhile there were the first attempts to break into broadcasting, too. Story played truant from Marconi's to sit in script conference for the popular radio comedy programme "Take it from Here", which starred Jimmy Edwards. He learned from this experience something that he would have to live with in his later film and television work - that very often nothing of what a scriptwriter produces is actually used. But he was also submitting plays and short stories while still at Marconi's, and this led to his first Thursday Play acceptance. Unfortunately the play - it had a little-girl-lost-on-a-bus theme - was broadcast in the afternoon, at a time when Jack was supposed to be taking pH measurements in Battersea Power Station. No one of course had a radio in there, but he managed to slip out onto the streets at the right time in search of a set. He frantically tried one shop after another, until a man selling musical instruments (drums predominantly) produced an ancient model from a back room.

"Hold this wire," the man said. Then the two of them bent to listen to a loud crackling, with just the occasional word breaking through. At last the shopkeeper asked, with some eagerness:

"Is it a cricket match?"

Later, back at the factory, Jack found his colleagues full of congratulation; they had been permitted a kind of ceremonial mass-listening. He was luckier with his first broadcast short stories, which were included in a country-life series.

A friend of Jack's until about this time was George Hoffman. He was from the same Cambridge, Pye Radio roots, and even less suited to industrial life. "Friend of the Famous" was the title of a *Guardian* piece Jack wrote about him. Hoffman had the same face and physique, the same big moustache and rolling eyes, as Jerry Calonna, whose chief claim to fame was a capacity to hold a single note until - well, as Jack puts it, you had to breathe for him. It was Hoffman's hope one day to walk in on Calonna and say, "Snap!" He had no technical training for anything and was employed by Marconi's as a "progress chaser". Anything that was needed and was difficult - and just about everything was difficult in those post-war austerity years - it was his job to find. But his *real* life - expensively attired in the best suits, shirts, ties and hand-made shoes - was spent in pursuit of the celebrities of the West End. A monthly visit to London's best night spots to rub shoulders with the likes of Ted Ray, Arthur Tracy and Jimmy

Edwards, absorbed almost his entire Marconi wage. George Hoffman was lucky to achieve two of his life-time ambitions: Jimmy Edwards made him a member of the "Handlebar Club", and he managed in New York to have himself photographed side-by-side with Jerry Colonna, their eyes rolling in opposite directions.

In 1950 Jack dedicated his third accepted novel, *Protection for a Lady,* a crime story set in New Orleans in the twenties' era of prohibition and jazz, to George Hoffman. He asked Jimmy Edwards to pass on a copy to him, but then shortly after that he heard that Hoffman had unexpectedly died under the anaesthetic during an ulcer operation. Jack himself has long had a dread of anaesthetics - for good medical reasons in his case; but also, one imagines, because of what happened all those years ago to poor George, who did not live long enough to become famous in his own right.

To complete the list of Jack's children by Evelyn (and backtrack a little on the domestic and love lives), Jenny had been born in 1945, and finally, two years later, came Caroline. She had the distinction of being born at Brocket Hall, a maternity home at this time but once the home of Byron's mistress Lady Caroline Lamb. Jack claims his daughter was born in the actual room - though not the very bed - of Caroline Lamb. Certainly she was named after the famous and wayward lady.

Bizarrely, though, Evelyn was visited as she recovered from the birth by the new lovers Jack and Ross together. One wonders what the nurses and other patients made of this, never mind Evelyn herself. Jack does seem to have been extraordinarily insensitive. It is not inconceivable, however, that Evelyn was thinking quietly to herself, "No more of this, thank God!"

But there was more to this visit than the mere fact of it. In *Dwarf Goes to Oxford,* in addition to the outdoor sexual adventures already touched on, Jack tells us that he made love to Ross under a hedge in the grounds of Brocket Hall as they waited to go in. One can see how the thought that soon they would be chatting with his wife and admiring the new baby as if nothing had happened could have provided the extra stimulus he sometimes needed.

Story has no regrets about having fathered so many children, but he confesses that his sexual bungling was the chief cause of it. With his wandering concentration, contraceptives were something he couldn't cope with. And in those days working-class women like Evelyn were less involved in birth-control procedures and thus at the mercy of their husbands or lovers. "Only men who can't do it have big families," is how Jack sums it up.

After Caroline came Lee, but this time Ross was of course the mother. In one of Jack's ever-discursive personal letters (just unearthed) I find I have some detail of the circumstances attending the *conception* of this particular baby. It happened in Ross's flat, just prior to her move into the Story household. As they were beginning to make love they heard a man whistling in the fog outside - not in appreciation; he was simply a passer-by. The whistling came closer and closer, and then began to recede, finally vanishing at just the moment when Lee was "planted". Candid as his letters can be, I can't tell if the passing presence of the phantom whistler made the crucial difference between success and failure on that foggy night long ago; though I fancy it did - to be remembered.

Extraordinarily tolerant as she was, it is surely doubtful if Evelyn knew Jack's girlfriend was expecting when she accepted her into the household. Ross herself may not have known. But when with the passing of the months the fact became clear and the time approached, it seems to have been plain to everyone that the limit had been reached. Even a man as unconventional as Jack Trevor Story couldn't face emerging from the same front door with two different families. And not only was Ross (from whose unpublished autobiography much of what follows is in outline taken) faced once more with homelessness; for the present she wouldn't be able to work, either. Jack could not support a second, independent family, so she did the only thing possible in the circumstances - went back to her mum. This was a very difficult step, for the old lady had an implacable and scarcely groundless hatred for Jack, whom she would only refer to as "that man". All of his very considerable charm had not only failed to win her round, it had made no impression at all on the strength of her hostility. She loathed him. Nor was he much better liked by Ross's sisters, from one of whom she became permanently estranged because of Jack. And his inability to provide at all adequately for his new son must have further damaged his reputation with the family, if that were possible. Little Lee turned out to be an energetic baby, too, and a considerable handful. Nevertheless, as soon as she was able, Ross had to find a job, leaving her aging mother to cope during the daytime with the difficult infant unaided.

Jack might have been expected to find this a satisfactory arrangement, except perhaps for some troubling of conscience; but he was by no means contented. He has a broad streak of paranoia in his nature, not so far seen in this story. Now it was about to erupt. He liked to have his women under control, but Ross, working again, was free to consort with other men. This drove him wild. An example of the jealous rages to come happened one afternoon when she was standing innocently outside her new place of work with her boss, admiring his new car. Jack suddenly appeared and dragged her roughly away, accusing her publicly of planning to drive off with the man to have sex with him; an idea which to Ross (so at any rate she says in her book) seemed fantastic. And he was angry about the baby, too, which he was unable to see so long as the boy was locked away at her mother's place. One evening he turned up in menacing mood demanding to see his son, and even threatening to take him away. It says something for his lack of physical resolve that the old lady - in angry mood herself of course - was able to eject him bodily from the house single-handed, while Ross ran upstairs to protect the sleeping child.

But it must be said that Ross evidently did not find this behaviour altogether unappealing. It was surely proof that he really loved her. She was still seeing him outside the house, and believed that his rage boiled down to a desire to live with her and the baby. Furthermore, he was prepared now to leave Evelyn and the other kids to do it. The tantrums and recriminations grew more violent until at last it seemed to Ross that only by complying with his demands would there be any peace. Her mother, too, left alone to look after the baby for much of the time now, and knowing bitterly that her daughter was seeing "that man" at every opportunity, was approaching the limit of *her* endurance. One late night, following a prolonged verbal battle with Jack, Ross found her mother ready for a showdown. Unable to face this, she broke a window on the landing with her fist in sheer frustration, then locked herself in her bedroom, leaving her mother to clear up the mess. Next morning she left the house abruptly, without a word, and kept an early appointment with Jack at the offices of an estate agent.

In the midst of this domestic and emotional turmoil, Jack was moving steadily, though without quite knowing it, towards the status of full-time writer. In his career at Marconi's he had begun in Special Products, under W B Bartley; then moved through Development Testing, Design, and on into technical writing. After a year of this he had an itch to put technical matters behind him altogether and work instead for Publicity, specifically on the company magazine, *The Marconi Companies and Their People*. Publicity was under the ultimate control of the Scientific Personnel Director. An interview was arranged for Jack with this exalted personage, for which he had to travel into London, where the man had his office. *The Trouble with Harry* was about to be published, and he had with him the first jacket "pull". They discussed his technical writing and spare-time efforts, and the director was impressed enough to offer him the job on the house journal he desired. But Jack might have got rather more out of the encounter had he appreciated more quickly who the director was, for with his weakness for faces he had failed to recognise him.

"I write books, too," the man said at length.

"Oh yes," said Jack "What name do you write under?"

To be fair, when I discussed this episode with him I had some difficulty in grasping the connection between Marconi Instruments and the chief book critic of the *Sunday Times* and famous author of *Strangers and Brothers,* C P Snow. (Evidently it was some kind of Government appointment.) So one can understand how Jack could have been bemused by the sudden discovery that he was talking to one of his favourite writers.

One morning a year or so later a letter arrived from Story's agent with the information that an American film producer (no name was mentioned) had made an offer of five hundred dollars for the film rights to *The Trouble with Harry.* He quickly asked one or two independent people what they thought of this and was advised that it was probably just an option. He requested his agent to check. She did, and back came the message (in those days all this had to be done by post) that no, this was very definitely the film rights; and furthermore a quick decision was needed. Still there was no clue as to who the producer might be. "Better accept it," she advised. "No one else is going to film the book, and five hundred dollars is five hundred dollars." (In point of fact five hundred dollars was little more than a hundred pounds at that time.) As ever, Story was short of money, with an overdraft and other debts. Now, out of the blue, some relief was on offer from these pressures. Further delay would be madness; he decided to accept.

Next a dozen copies of the contract arrived, driving him for the moment unexpectedly into further debt, for each required a two-dollar stamp. The stamps had to be obtained from the American embassy on Grosvenor Square, and to pay for them he had to borrow money from his publishers, T V Boardman. And on top of that, of course, was the return postage.

When he heard later that rights for the book were in the hands of Alfred Hitchcock (a huge name, of course, even in those pre-*Psycho* days), Story naturally felt cheated; and now, whenever *The Trouble with Harry* is revived or shown on television, he is reminded of the deception. But of course he bears no burning grudge, for he recognizes that to have had his first published novel bought by Hitchcock was a piece of almost unbelievable good fortune, the money scarcely relevant. Later it would open doors for him into the film world; in 1951 it was enough to convince him that the moment had arrived to take the big step and become a professional writer.

This was also approximately the moment when Ross walked out on her mother. She was enjoying quite a bit of success with her own books at that time, having moved on a little from her westerns into more general novels, though still with an American setting. Her chief worry had been how she could work and look after Lee at the same time, but Jack had convinced her that they could make a go of it as writers. He had several hundred pounds due to him from Marconi's pension fund, and the firm had agreed to continue to use him on the house journal for a period while he found his feet as a writer. The prospects seemed quite good. The estate agent offered them a large semi-detached house in quite a pleasant part of St Albans, with lawns and flowerbeds front and back. There seemed to Ross no reason why they should not be happy there.

But Jack's jealous rages did not subside as she had logically expected, now that she was no longer going out to work and mixing with other men. If anything, they grew worse. He still of course had his other family in Welwyn Garden City, and had no intention of making a clean break. He would never leave Evelyn completely (as indeed later he would never turn his back finally on Ross). This meant that his movements were unpredictable, so Ross couldn't easily settle into a routine. And much worse than that, whenever he turned up at the house she had to face a grilling over whether she had been out, whom she had seen or spoken to, what they had said - and with violence to come (though usually against objects in the house rather than the personal kind), if he was dissatisfied with the answers. It was impossible for her to write, and she began to dread the sound of his ancient little Austin drawing up outside. Then to cap it all she found herself pregnant again.

This new baby (Jack's seventh) was born at home, all in rather a rush, with the father missing and Ross's mother in attendance. Next day he called in, but only long enough to give the little girl the name Janet. (Later, Ross was able to change it to the one she had chosen: Lindsay.) But now, she thought, Jack would surely quieten down at last, since no other man in his right mind could possible have designs on a thirty-five year old woman saddled with a misbehaving toddler and a baby in a pram. There was to be no relief, however. Little more than a week after the birth, Ross's mother having left, there was a routine visit by the estate agent, who was evidently in control of the mortgage. Ross let this slip when Jack next appeared and launched into his usual interrogation. Seeing her mistake, she quickly added that there had been a woman with him. Jack saw that this was a lie - which it was - and Ross's punishment was to have her head banged roughly against the wall. Then he filled a bowl in the kitchen with icy cold water, and threw it over her. Later, learning that she had to keep an appointment with her doctor for a post-natal examination, he put all of her clothes - every stich - into the bath and filled it with water, to prevent her leaving the house. (Shades of his maternal grandfather, Sam Dyball!) Ross thought nothing worse could happen, but a few weeks later, after another quarrel, he entered the house when she was out with Lee and Lindsay and did a systematic wrecking job on the furniture and carpets. When she returned she was relieved to see him driving off, but the mood lasted only a moment. The children were hungry, and the shock of seeing what he had done to their home was followed by the amazing discovery that all the cupboards were bare. Everything edible had been removed,

along with bedding, towels and other necessities. She thought
he must have taken it all away in the back of his car; but when
he came back, full of the most abject contrition, an hour later
she found that he had worked like a demon to bundle
everything into the loft. In this mood she could order him to do
her bidding. Late into the night, having brought the stuff down
again and put it back where it belonged, he was still tacking
down the stair carpet.

All sexual partnerships have their stormy moments; even so,
except as fits of temporary insanity, these actions are hard to
account for. This is very much Ross's side of the story (and
there is more to come), but Jack has confirmed the general
outline of these events. At the same time, Ross's memoir is
sometimes less than candid. She makes no mention, for
instance, of the period when she consented to live at the house
on Meadway with Evelyn. But she certainly intended the book
(which was written not long before her death from cancer in
1980) to be published, so she is unlikely to have been
excessively inventive.

   If stress was a factor in his behaviour, then Jack was
certainly under a lot of that now. Earning a living as a writer
was proving to be no piece or cake. Though published, his
novels brought in very little (they scarcely repaid the
publisher's advance); while his short stories earned a good deal
more in relation to their content, but had the disadvantage that
he had to write at least a dozen for every acceptance.
Television and film work lay ahead, but in the meantime he was
only able to scratch a living by taking on what he calls "potato-
picking" jobs. All more or less simultaneously, he read novels
for MGM at thirty shillings a time (the work couldn't be
skimped because a detailed synopsis of each novel had to be
prepared); did a short-story editing job for *John Bull*, for
similar pay; worked for various cheap romance magazines (he
used to compose both questions and answers for *Love Letters*);
and for the pulp market wrote thrillers and westerns under such

aliases as Rex Riotti and Brett Harding. Here he was close to the murky world of fifties-style pornography - Scion and Panther books - and such celebrated writers in the genre as Hank Janson (real name Steve Francis), a notorious fugitive who had to live in Spain and could only make clandestine visits to London when the police were looking the other way.

The "Mr Big" behind this operation was a Jewish gentleman called Mr Emmanuel. "I demand of my authors a fuck every fourth page," he used to tell his new recruits. It was a profitable business, but risky, and around the time when Jack Trevor Story came on the pulp scene he was looking to improve his publishing image. Jack had had a few stories in the *London Mystery Magazine,* which was respectable. Mr Emmanuel bought it, then contacted Jack to ask what he would "charge" to edit the magazine. They met in Kensington Gardens, where they had a strolling conversation, in the course of which Mr Emmanuel, hands clasped behind his back, outlined his plans for buying up much of the London publishing world. "On Thursday I buy Secker & Warburg," he confided, while Jack tried to think of a suitable figure to charge the man for the post he was offering. In the end he failed to drive a hard bargain; the wage was modest, and even in combination with the fitful earnings from the rest of his frenetic literary work not enough still for two families to live on.

It seemed certain that he would have to abandon professional authorship and creep back to his job at Marconi's; but then suddenly to the rescue came none other than England's most famous detective after Sherlock Holmes, the legendary Sexton Blake.

Chapter Seven

THE TWO-FAMILY PARENT

Certain years Jack Trevor Story describes as definitive; 1954 was one such.

It was the year England won back the Ashes, Dennis Compton scoring the winning runs; though national sporting triumphs tended to be lost on Jack. He certainly wouldn't remember the day were it not for the fact that on the very afternoon of the victory he had a story - one of his well-turned short shorts - in the *Evening News*. Copies were selling at the street corners at a furious rate, and for an excited moment he half imagined that his own modest contribution might be causing the fever.

But 1954 is better remembered as the year of a highly fortuitous encounter that has over time acquired the status of a minor legend. It happened towards Christmas time - always a testing time for the literary potato-picker, who had two homes to think about now and a multitude of children, all hungry for something more than just the basics of existence. The situation always seemed most hopeless as the Season of Goodwill approached, and in this particular year it was worse than ever. But then he bumped into Bill Howard Baker in Trafalgar Square.

He had met Baker in the offices of Panther Books, where he worked as an editor. The establishment was owned (or part-owned, or soon-to-be-owned) by Mr Emmanuel; and he it was who took Jack along to meet the staff at some point in their negotiations over duties and charges. In fact Mr Emmanuel had half a mind to move Baker out and install Story as editor; but there were plans, too, to raise Panther's image, and a different kind of editor would be needed for that. This eventually was the course adopted, so that not only was Story not offered that particular editorship; Bill Baker found himself (some time later) out of a job anyway.

Baker had heard that Amalgamated Press were looking for a suitable editor to take over the moribund Sexton Blake Library. He applied, and was offered the position provided he could produce - in a hurry - a new, original Sexton Blake thriller for a re-launch. It was a task he felt unable to manage without assistance, desperate as he was to have the job. Wrestling with the problem, he wandered into Trafalgar Square, and there met an equally despondent Jack Trevor Story. His luck was certainly in that day, for Jack maintains that this was one of the very few times in his life when he has actually walked across Trafalgar Square. He likes to avoid doing *anything* that conventional people might be drawn to, as a rule.

Explaining his own plight, Baker suggested a collaboration. Perhaps from having spent too much time in the airless offices of the leading pornographers of the day, he declared that he could only manage indoor scenes; outdoor life was something of a closed book to him. Some of Jack's best moments had been in the open air, so he was happy to do either. They agreed to do alternate chapters, switching the setting from indoors to out. Many famous authors of detective stories - Agatha Christie, Leslie Charteris, Edgar Wallace - had written Sexton Blakes in their time; but none of their work was to hand. All the collaborators had to go on was a story by Rex Stout involving gypsies, kidnapping, and two characters called Pedro and Tinker. But they were both professionals, and somehow an acceptable thriller emerged from the blankness. Bill Baker got the job of reviving the fortunes of Sexton Blake and his chums (later he took over the character entirely and published new Sexton Blakes in much improved hardback editions); and this in turn led to a handy outlet for Jack's own rejected manuscripts, old and new, at a very useful hundred-and-fifty pounds a time. He developed a facility for switching stories back and forth from Sexton Blake to general thriller, often by little more than changes of name and profession. This is why, if you read those tatty paper-backs (his description), with their lurid covers and tiny double-column printing, you sometimes get the feeling that Sexton Blake and his team are hardly central to the action.

Mr Emmanuel's pulp philosophy was that what was in the book scarcely mattered; the covers were all important. "They are for lorry drivers to pin up in their cabins," he would explain. Even so, Jack's approach to thriller writing was highly professional. It is tempting to think that he must have been writing down to his readers, but in point of fact these books - like everything else he has ever written - were the best he could do at the time. And Bill Baker took what was between the covers a good deal more seriously than did Mr Emmanuel. "Don't forget your little homily," he used to say, referring to Jack's favourite way of opening a story. His 1969 novel *Dishonourable Member* begins with these words:

> There is a sadness which grows from the seeds of remembered happiness; there is a weariness which springs unrequested from the remembered fountains of youth; there is a nostalgia conjured from faraway places and gone people and moments which have long since ticked into the infinite fog.

That's fine for a novel which was reviewed as literature; but one wonders what the lorry drivers made of it more than a decade earlier, for it was lifted without alteration from a Sexton Blake. (As indeed was the entire novel, except that Sexton Blake became an MP.) Or again, take the closing words of *Company of Bandits*:

> A silence grew in the softly-lighted room and traffic noises from Baker Street came remotely as though from another time. Mrs Bardell's departure did nothing to disturb the illusion of the softer yesterdays of the old building. And the dog entering dropped and melted

silent as snow into the warmest, reddest glow of
firelight.

Story was free between those lurid covers to experiment with
philosophical or poetic writing. But the exercise also forced
him to create characters and devise plots under pressure, and to
write at much greater length than he had lately been
accustomed to, turning him into a true professional. Nor was it
a case of casting pearls before swine, for the quality of Story's
Sexton Blakes did not go unnoticed. Over the years they
caught the attention of readers more discerning than the fifties'
lorry drivers, and indeed have become admired collector's
items. Here is Alan Forrest, writing in *Books and Bookmen* in
the seventies:

> If you do own any old Sexton Blakes, search them for
> Story titles. Grapple them to you with hoops of steel . . .

As I write, Bill Howard Baker has recently died. The lengths
of the obituary notices in the newspapers testify to the
importance and high regard he came to have in publishing. His
chief work was in keeping alive the old Greyfriars characters
from the pre-war *Magnet* and *Gem*. This was a mission that
had Jack Trevor Story's full sympathy, for (William Saroyan's
influence notwithstanding) he sees himself very much as an
extension of the Frank Richards, P G Wodehouse, Evelyn
Waugh tradition in English letters.
  1954 was the year Sexton Blake saved him from
ignominious return to Marconi's, but it was in that same
definitive year that Jack's eighth child and Ross's third - Lorel -
was born.

Lorel would turn a difficult life into a nightmare; but in the
period leading up to this final unplanned birth, living in
circumstances some way removed from the mellow warmth of
Sexton Blake's Baker Street flat, Ross (and here I am dipping

into her unpublished autobiography again) was finding it hard to keep up her side of the writing partnership. Under constant pressure from Jack, she did manage to finish one book, however. It was a further departure from the sort of thing her publishers (Herbert Jenkins) were used to, but she had high hopes for it, not least because the money problems were so acute. Alas, at just the moment when the need to pay off the mortgage arrears on the St Albans house was most compelling, a stunning letter arrived telling her that Herbert Jenkins were not going to take the novel. Unlike Jack, Ross had till then experienced very little rejection. Now in desperation she offered to rewrite her story; but all the publishers wanted from her was more westerns, and she had nothing to hand. The mortgage arrears as a consequence couldn't be met, and soon they received notice to quit.

Homelessness faced Ross and her children once again (Jack of course had his second home in Welwyn Garden City). She appealed once more to her mother, who again offered a roof and a bed, though with "that man" obviously excluded. But Jack claimed to have written to his own mother, up in Cambridge, who, he said, would take them all in. Their possessions were piled into the little Austin and without any formal contact with the estate agent they headed north.

When Jack insisted on parking some distance from the house and entering alone, Ross was mortified. It was clear that he hadn't consulted his mother at all, but was relying on her customary generous nature. Somehow space was found for them in the little council house in Chesterton: Lee's cot was erected on the tiny landing space, while Lindsay slept in her pram, jammed into a corner alongside the gas-stove in the kitchen. Each night Jack and Ross (or more usually Ross alone) had to unroll a mattress from the stair cupboard and lay it under the kitchen table. In fact the house had two bedrooms, and things might have been easier had it not been for Rhoda's sinister lodger, Mrs Bannell.

Mrs Bannell had been in residence for some time, and was a troublesome fixture. Rhoda complained constantly about the woman, but always stopped short of any direct action to remove her - doubtless because she needed the money; although she was still managing to do some work in the colleges. Mrs Bannell allowed no one to know anything about her life at all. Except for infrequent visits to the kitchen to fill her kettle, she kept herself to her bedroom, which was known to contain no ornaments or personal nick-nacks of any kind. It even lacked a chair; apparently she ate her mysterious meals sitting on her bed. Each morning before leaving for work, she stripped the bedding off and locked everything away in a cupboard. So ascetic was her domestic regimen that she even refused electricity and moved about at night with only the light of a candle - a potential fire risk that worried Rhoda to death. In the small hours she could be heard opening her cupboard and dragging out what sounded like an enormous trunk.

Rhoda herself seems to have been something of a changed character from the enterprising young widow of earlier times, although there are conflicting views. Jacqueline and Jenny remember her as being a fairly inactive person in their childhood years, memorable chiefly for dosing herself constantly with indigestion powder. Jack speaks of her as always a proud woman, of upright bearing still, who was quite a disciplinarian so far as the grand-children were concerned, insisting that all toys and games must be returned to their proper place after use. Ross by contrast portrays her as a big, sagging woman with red-rimmed eyes, who was very deaf and used a cumbersome hearing aid that sometimes emitted whistling noises, besides having a loudly rumbling stomach.

Even so, Ross was not unhappy in her new lodgings. Having effectively lost her own family, she was in need of new family ties; and just as she had struck up a good relationship with Jack's wife Evelyn, so now she began to meet and like his Cambridge people, after some initial resentment when they called around one by one to size her up. With Elsa, she seems to have got on particularly well. Despite the cramped living conditions, all this represented an improvement in her life - when Jack wasn't around.

He was sleeping during the week (most nights anyway) in Welwyn Garden City and travelling into London each day to work for Mr Emmanuel. As a rule he only came up to Cambridge at the weekends, and this was certainly enough for both Ross and Rhoda, for there was no sign of his jealous rages abating even now. The moment he arrived there would be the usual menacing question-and-answer session, and he had even begun to seek confirmation of Ross's replies from Lee, who was growing wary of him too. Sometimes he arrived drunk, and then the scenes would be worse than ever, with ornaments flying, Rhoda screaming, and the neighbours out in the street. Elsa came into the firing line - accused of turning Ross against him. So concerned were she and her mother that Ross might suffer serious injury that she asked a policeman friend to patrol in the vicinity whenever Jack was expected. Rhoda meanwhile had confided to Ross that Jack as a teenager had once tried to stab her with a carving knife for, as he thought, carrying on with a lodger. Sometimes she had thought him mad.

Ross wondered once more if life with her mother at Bricket Wood might not be better - *safer*, at any rate - and wrote to her again. She must have told Jack about this, for he kept an eye on the post and happened to be there to intercept - and withhold - the reply when it came. Ross was puzzled not to receive an answer, and might have been kept in ignorance of the deception had her mother not died of a heart-attack just a few weeks later. Then Jack confessed, and she found that her mother had responded warmly to her plea and agreed to have her and the children back once again.

Ross's father had died before her mother, so the Bricket Wood house could be sold and the money divided. This brought relief for a while from the money problems and meant that she and Jack could go house-hunting once more. She had grown to like

Cambridge, but they would have to move sometime. The new house they settled on was in the much less attractive town of Harpenden, but conveniently close to Welwyn Garden City. This would ease Jack's shuttling problems, which were so much a feature of his life in the fifties. The house was called Meynell Cottage (after the poetess Kate Meynell). It consisted in fact of two cottages knocked into one and was quite large. In the garden was a shed, in which from the evidence hats had rather incredibly been manufactured. But Ross found the atmosphere of Meynell Cottage gloomy. In fact she writes in her autobiography that she was approaching the unhappiest period of her life.

Christmas was near, and Ross had expected to remain in Cambridge. Jack insisted at the last minute, however, that they move with the children to their new home to spend Christmas there. This presented Ross with sudden practical problems of the kind men never think of - buying food, and more importantly presents of some kind for the children. To avoid a scene, she agreed to go along with his idea, resolved to try to make the best of it. But no sooner had they arrived than Jack declared that he would have to go over to Welwyn Garden City to organise Evelyn. He didn't return until Boxing Day, so that Ross and the children had to spend their first Christmas in their gloomy new home alone, with almost nothing to make the occasion festive. It was a bad fresh start.

The money from the sale of her mother's house gave them only temporary financial respite. Within a year they were back in debt, Jack having foolishly given up his regular editing job in London. The dining-room suite was repossessed, followed by the cooker, though the men from the Gas Board at least had the grace to allow Ross to finish cooking a meal before they began to disconnect it. The Austin had been replaced by a newer Hillman saloon, but this too was on hire-purchase and soon had to go, leaving them now dependent on public transport and scratching around for coppers for even the shortest journey. At this new low point, the ubiquitous Mr Simpson, of Jack's Pye

Radio and Marconi Instruments days, turned up as a temporary benefactor. Jack met him by chance in the town and discovered he was living in the next street. He became a very frequent visitor, and even installed his workbench in their garden shed. Mr Simpson was still inclined to stand on his head at unexpected moments; it was some kind of yoga exercise. Often this would happen without warning in their living room, in the midst of a casual visit. Whatever this obsessive practice was doing to Mr Simpson's brains, it had both good and bad results for Jack and Ross. On the plus side, for a time he handed over to them his family-allowance money, obviously intended to benefit his own children; but then when they were making tentative plans to sell Meynell Cottage, he claimed to have a permanent lien on the shed and was able to block the idea. This brought the curious friendship to an abrupt end, though Mr Simpson continued of course to crop up unexpectedly in Jack's life for many years. After this the court bailiff became a regular visitor - almost replacing Mr Simpson as a family friend - in connection with various summonses and repossessions, though somehow they managed to remain in the house. One day when they had no money at all they discovered an old set of golf clubs in the rafters of the garage. Jack contacted the local golf club, who offered a pound for them. The hunt for coppers to make the necessary bus trip on this occasion involved lifting floor boards where a stray penny was thought to have been lost.

Jack came in one evening with the news that Panther Books wanted westerns and would pay sixty pounds per manuscript. He persuaded Ross to allow him to re-type certain of her books, with a few minor name changes and other revisions, and present them as originals, confident that the deception would never be discovered. But Herbert Jenkins found out somehow, and Ross, who had been their top western writer, was struck off their list of authors. Jack eventually admitted total guilt to the firm, but they had taken the step of hiring another western writer and she was out for good. She never received another penny from them. (Jack's version of this is that he didn't know the books were copyright.)

This was yet another low point - just when it seemed things could not get worse, they always did. And the very next blow was that Ross found she was pregnant again. Lorel.

Doubtless the house on Meadway in Welwyn Garden City was full of the same effort to make ends meet. Things there may well have been even more desperate, but Evelyn of course was not a writer so there is no parallel record. Poverty there certainly was, with bailiffs as family friends; but no one I have spoken to remembers any scenes of emotional drama to compare with what was happening in the Ross family. Evelyn was placid and uncomplaining, resigned to having a husband who came and went as he pleased and would always return even when it seemed certain that he had gone forever. All other parts of his life being so stressful, it may be that he saw the Meadway house as a comparative haven of rest and quiet, notwithstanding the five kids. His prolonged absences must have been the subject of local gossip, but in spite of what the neighbours had already seen - Ross living in the house and leaving pregnant - this seems to have been relatively mild. His daughters (by Evelyn) can remember the reputation he had for charm and how unknown ladies would stop them on the street to enquire how their father was. (One wonders what kind of tale he had been telling them.) His sons-in-law tend to the belief that he ought to have made a clean break, but looking back the daughters certainly preferred having a dad who went missing for long periods to having no dad at all. Elsa remembers them as happy children, in spite of their state of near-destitution. They had no fear of their father - Caroline used to let down the tyres of his car to try to get him to stay - and grew up much less bitter about the effect his behaviour had on their early lives than might have been feared. This undoubtedly was Evelyn's doing. Deeply hurt as she must have been, she managed somehow not to turn the children against their father, who one day she secretly hoped would come back to stay. How long she sustained this hope is impossible to say. In later life, engrossed in watching wrestling on television, she would scarcely notice him when he put in one of his infrequent Saturday afternoon appearances. "Don't make any crumbs," she might call, hearing him searching for something to eat in the kitchen, for she had by then become very house proud. Since her death in 1978, Jack misses Evelyn simply as someone to visit when bored; and yet even when the children had grown up and there were other women whom he might have married, he wouldn't divorce her. She died in his arms.

Ross was not strong on dates; they tend to be a male obsession. Her manuscript continues for page after page, chapter after chapter, with scarcely a clue as to even the approximate year. From her account, an awful lot seems to have happened between Jack's decision to leave Marconi's and the arrival of Lorel, which I know was only three years later. Jack is better on years; definitive ones at any rate. His weakness tends to be decades, with confusion in particular between the fifties and sixties. So there is no guarantee that the chronology of events as I am relating them is precisely accurate, since I have no other sources when it comes to that kind of detail.

Jack is quite certain that Lorel was born in 1954, even though he had no interest in either the pregnancy or the birth. His love for Ross - or whatever the emotion was that caused his insanely jealous behaviour - was in decline and he was on the lookout for girlfriends again; if indeed he had ever given up this compulsive searching.

Ross was old now for having babies, nearly forty, but she had no anxiety about the likely health of this third child. And although Jack's lack of support and concern was upsetting, Lorel turned out to be an attractive and normal baby, by all appearances. As she began to grow she proved to be very strong-willed and infuriatingly uncooperative in the routine baby procedures like eating, sleeping and nappy changing; but she wasn't yet the dominant worry in the household, only an irritating cause of sleeplessness. They remained chiefly preoccupied with trying to keep their heads above water financially.

A minor film producer called Mr Slome entered their lives around this time and became their friend and benefactor much as Mr Simpson had been. He was obsessed with a film idea involving the explosion of an atom bomb in South Africa. Mr Slome had the resources to engage Jack as a scriptwriter on a regular wage for a period, besides even providing food sometimes, along with help towards clothes for the children. But he was never able to sell his eccentric idea to his contacts in Wardour Street and the arrangement eventually fizzled out.

Another potential source of income was lodgers, or at least that was the plan. They were mostly unlucky with the people they took in. One very plausible couple delivered brand new furniture for their room and paid rent in advance by cheque, which in those days ought to have seemed suspicious. Ross had a remarkably trusting nature, however. It wasn't long before the police came around - actually before the couple had moved in. They were wanted in connection with a trail of bouncing cheques. The woman was the brains of the partnership, and it was she who went to prison. Ross took pity on her and wrote to her while she was locked up, with the result that on release she came back into their lives - with a baby, born in prison. The experience had evidently cured her criminal inclinations, though not her desire for easy money. She had a story to sell - having a baby in prison - and proceeded to try to interest the Sunday tabloids in it. Nowadays it doesn't seem much of a story, but in the fifties it was evidently sensational, for the *Sunday Pictorial* ran a big spread, even though she had in point of fact been allowed to enter an ordinary hospital for the birth itself so the baby wouldn't have a social stigma. Jack was astounded that money could be made so easily and tried to interest the press in Ross's western writing. Somehow, though, when it comes to making money he has always lacked the magic touch.

Late 1954, as already related, was an especially bad time. What with the extra baby, and all these other troubles, only the chance meeting with Bill Baker and the Sexton Blake possibilities it opened up spared Jack the embarrassment of returning to Marconi's. But Sexton Blake would only ever be for survival. In 1955 there came the prospect of a more significant lightening of the financial gloom with the release of Hitchcook's film of *The Trouble with Harry*.

Jack wasn't involved in any way with the making of the film, though he was pleased enough with the result. The locale was transplanted from the fringes of Welwyn Garden City to the splendour of the woods of Vermont ablaze with autumn colours, though the storyline followed his novel surprisingly closely. *The Trouble with Harry* gave Shirley Maclaine and John Forsythe their first important screen roles, but was a triumph especially for Edmund Gwenn as the Captain, even though he was seriously ill throughout the shooting and in fact died soon afterwards. It was a great box-office success, but brought Jack no immediate benefits. His potato-picking work continued much as before. One day, however, he heard that Alfred Hitchcock was in London, staying at Claridges. It happened that the bailiffs had arrived that day to remove a substantial part of the furniture from Meynell Cottage. Perhaps with some prompting from Ross, Jack saw an opportunity to touch Hitchcock for a few hundred pounds that very day and maybe save the furniture. He hoped, too, that it might be only an advance on a fairer settlement later.

"Lovely film, lovely film," said Hitchcock on the telephone when Jack rang him at Claridges. Then with his inimitable slow unbroken delivery he told Jack all about the terrible frustrations they had had, what with the need to wait for the leaves to change to just the right colours, and the problems with poor Edmund Gwenn. He was playing for time, of course, but at last Jack got an opportunity to ask politely about the prospect of more money, bearing in mind how little he had been paid and how much the film must be making.

"Oh, that would be most unethical," drawled Hitchcock, with only the customary amount of humour in his voice. "*Most* unethical . . . But I'll tell you what I'll do. Send me your next novel, and I'll buy it whether I use it or not. How does that sound?"

"I've got it right here, still in manuscript."

Hitchcock was evidently positive enough at this point to encourage Jack to seek a lift with the bailiff to Harpenden station. They drove down in the man's pick-up truck with all the furniture piled high on the back. This was in winter, close to Christmas again, and he was wearing a big Humphrey Bogart style raincoat with deep pockets, in one of which he had the rolled-up manuscript. Eventually he arrived at Claridges, only to be told that Mr Hitchcock and his entourage had left for the boat-train at Victoria. By the time he caught up with them Jack must have looked desperate. Hitchcock was surrounded by minders, ready to board the train. Jack explained his business between gasping breaths and reached deep into his pocket for the manuscript - whereupon the minders closed ranks around the portly figure to protect him. Everyone thought this wild and cheated writer was about to draw a gun.

Jack Trevor Story got no more money from Alfred Hitchcock that day; nor would he ever. He managed to hand over the manuscript, but it was returned with a standard rejection letter. Even so, this was an important moment in the opening up of his scriptwriting career, for Hitchcock's influential agent Bob Fenn had taken note of what had happened. He wrote to Jack, offering to represent him, and soon well-paid film work for directors and producers far more important then Mr Slome began to flood in.

He also broke into television at this point with a play in the *Love Birds* series - one of the very first on the new Independent

Television channel - in which a budgie provides a key piece of evidence in connection with a murder enquiry. And it was in connection with the screening of this play that he was able to invite into Meynell Cottage a young schoolteacher (female) whom he had met on a train. That in itself wasn't particulary suspicious, since by no means everyone had a television set then and it was not uncommon for people in that position to be invited into someone else's home to watch a particular programme. But of course Jack had other motives besides simply entertaining the girl. She was in need of lodgings, and following this innocent first meeting he was able to persuade Ross that they should take her in. Everyone says how sharp Ross was compared with Evelyn, but this looks like evidence of simple-mindedness, for by now they were seldom sleeping together and she knew Jack's record. Soon he had the girl installed tantalisingly in the back bedroom.

Maybe Ross thought this was the best way of keeping an eye on the two of them. Jack liked to work at night, always composing straight onto the typewriter. Ross probably found the racket comforting, for it told her precisely where he was and what he was doing. And she had further reassurance, if she was thinking about the possibility, that he would have to pass her bedroom to reach the new lodger's room. But Jack was in a romantic fever, and inventive enough to find a way around all this. He made a long tape recording of the sound of his typewriter, and set this playing while he stole out of the house and entered the girl's window with the aid of a makeshift ladder. Evidently he was expected, though from what Jack has said about it his cunning in reaching the girl's bed probably exceeded his performance when he got there, for he was once more in love.

If I have seemed to delay reaching the subject of Jack and Ross's third child, Lorel, it hasn't only been for suspense. Although now well into her thirties, Lorel remains a sensitive issue in the Story family. As already said, she was a difficult baby. With time, contrary to normal human expectation, she grew worse rather than better. Up to the age of four she spoke only once, despite having an obvious capacity to understand what was said to her. Four more years would pass before she spoke again. Ross devotes a chapter to her early development, or lack of it, which Jack printed in *Dwarf Goes to Oxford*. Her most characteristic activity as a baby was to rock continuously in her cot. This would propel it across the bedroom floor until an obstruction was reached, whereupon she would bang the cot rhythmically against the wall or furniture. Out of the cot, too, she often rocked incessantly, if only from one foot to the other. A photograph in Jack's book of Lorel as a toddler, held between Lee and Lindsay, is misleading for it seems she had no interest in playing with the other children. Nor for that matter would she play alone with toys. A strange case was Lorel in those days. There was a clear intelligence in her eyes, and yet she could neither be coaxed nor slapped into any sort of manageable cooperation. Trips to the shops were impossible with her, for she would tear off her clothes as fast as Ross tried to put them on. Nor would she consent to going in the car, so that the short motoring trips that had sometimes been possible when Jack was around also became a thing of the past. For a brief period she attended nursery school, but she was rejected as uncontrollable. Ross became a prisoner, at once bitter and full of guilt. The weirdest part of the girl's behaviour was her occasional habit of using Ross's hand to pick something up. This wasn't done because she couldn't manage; nor was there anything affectionate in it. She used the hand much as she might have used a mechanical implement. Nowadays, especially since the film *Rain Man*, her condition might have been recognised more quickly. She saw other people, even her parents, only as objects. Ross had seven years of struggle before a doctor finally diagnosed her as autistic.

So, where's the controversy? Jack was away for much of the time with his other commitments, so the childcare burden fell most heavily on Ross. But whether he was home or not, there would usually be typing going on. Ross would not permit herself to send out any manuscript that wasn't an "original", for instance, so that whenever she was asked for a copy she would have to type out the entire book again, albeit it at a furious speed, single-spaced. I don't suppose this was her most prolific period, but she wrote a great many books in her time (under a variety of pseudonyms), and in Lorel's infancy money was still very short. The child was only manageable in her cot, if the thump, thumping against the wall could be endured - and it happens that hammering away at an old-fashioned manual typewriter conveniently drowns all but the most intrusive background noise. With two other young children in the house, one can see how the suspicion could have grown that the little girl wasn't being properly cared for. Rhoda had always been an activist, writing to the newspapers and such on matters that aroused her feelings. Now, with Elsa's support, she reported the case to the NSPCC, whose officers visited the home. No action was ever taken, however, and Rhoda died soon afterwards (1957). But it wasn't the end of the controversy. Elsa would not accept that there was anything wrong with the child except emotional deprivation. She persisted in this opinion even after Lorel had been diagnosed as autistic by a doctor and had begun to be removed from her home environment, at first as a temporary arrangement, but soon - and to Ross's great relief, in spite of her guilt feelings - more permanently. When Lorel was twelve, Elsa effectively took over responsibility for her by removing her from an institution where she was (so Elsa claimed) being maltreated and taking her home to Cambridge, believing even at this late stage that the child might be cured by loving kindness. Ross and Jack meanwhile had moved from Harpenden to Worthing. Over the years, at no little personal sacrifice, Elsa appears at least to have succeeded in establishing a kind of rapport with Lorel. But having her permanently at home has proved impossible in the end, since her behaviour remains unpredictable, and even on occasion dangerous.

I don't have the views of Lee or Lindsay, but Jenny (one of Jack's daughters by Evelyn), who has had some experience of it in her work, accepts that emotional deprivation could have been a factor in Lorel's condition. As for Jack himself, he believes that Elsa's opinion of the matter is misguided, while of course being grateful to her for everything she has tried to do to improve Lorel's quality of life.

When I visited Elsa in connection with this book I pointed out to her that there was a chapter in *Dwarf Goes to Oxford* on Lorel, written by her mother. She seemed unaware of this, so I took the book off the shelf and showed it to her.

"Did she read it?" Jack asked me later.

"Well, not immediately."

"No - she won't, either," he said.

I find I have entered just a tiny way into the controversy myself, since in spite of my protestations that I wish only to be objective, Jack suspects that I lean privately towards Elsa's view.

"You don't know what Ross went through with that baby," he will say, when in fact I can imagine only too clearly how bad it must have been. I am more struck by his habit of referring to Lorel as having been a problem for Ross alone.

He published a piece about her in the *Sunday Times* some years ago with the title "Who is My Daughter?". It produced a large response, mainly hostile. Only correspondents who had personal or professional experience of autistic children responded sympathetically.

Chapter Eight

LIVE NOW, PAY LATER

The book that Hitchcock turned down was called *The Money Goes Round and Round*, published in 1958 by Alvin Redman. It was Jack Trevor Story's first non-Sexton Blake novel for some years. Readers who have perhaps been a little baffled by his later writings, and who may even suspect him of being some kind of literary charlatan, ought to turn to his early books. They will find them to be models of clear, concise prose. Back then he was a thorough professional, able to turn his hand to virtually any kind of literary composition and to produce a result that was accessible to readers at all levels. The increasingly personal and idiosyncratic writing style and unsignposted storytelling method of his later period are built on very solid foundations.

The Money Goes Round and Round is therefore no literary masterpiece, but simply a highly readable story, buoyant in spirit and pleasantly humorous without being screamingly funny (achievement enough when you reflect that it must have been written just as the problems with Lorel were emerging). It concerns a detective writer, Arthur Taverner, who is unpopular at home but for some reason a tremendous commercial success in Spain. The problem is that he is unable to bring his accumulating royalties into England because of currency regulations, so he and his wife Mildred, who live like paupers for most of the year, must visit Spain from time to time to try to spend the money. But even the most concentrated extravagant living makes little impression on their Spanish wealth, and besides, they don't much care for the country. How to get the money home is the question, and it happens that Arthur has reached a similar impasse in his latest detective novel. He already has a fictional solution, but one of his artistic principles is that every plot device in his stories must be possible in real life. When in doubt he likes to try things out. The happily married pair always journey down to Spain by car. Arthur's fictional scheme, which he now plans to put to the test, is to fill the tyres with banknotes . . .

Story dedicated the book to "my creditors". He had no foreign currency holdings himself, accessible or otherwise, and any money that it might earn was already spoken for. But the title of his soon-to-be-published new novel did at least raise a laugh during one of his frequent appearances at the county court in connection with mortgage arrears or other debts. In fact he must have been at just the point then of breaking into big money at last as a film scriptwriter; although he wasn't to know that, and it might not in any case have carried any more plausibility. Not that he was seen by the courts simply as a dissolute character who could not be believed. One friendly judge used to direct the court to accept Mr Story's word whenever he detected scepticism in a lawyer's remarks. He could be his own worst enemy, however. At a later bankruptcy hearing, when asked to explain how he could have spent such a large sum so quickly, he said, "You know how it is, Judge, twenty or two hundred, it always lasts a week to a fortnight."

Missing, certainly, from these many court appearances was any sense of the kind of shame that would overwhelm more conventional souls. Jack Trevor Story has never known, or at any rate cared a damn for the opinions of people who think in terms of social disgrace, although practical matters such as the size of a likely fine have been important to him, sometimes desperately so. If anything, his court appearances have been good for his image, he feels. (They continue down to the present day.)

At the time of Bob Fenn's intervention, Story was already familiar with many of the British film studios, for he had worked as a contract writer for them all at one time or another right from the beginning of his professional career, writing synopses of novels and doing odd scripting jobs whenever the opportunity arose - films like *Son of Robin Hood*, which he believes had one of the Gabor sisters cast incongruously as Maid Marian. He had a strong natural talent, and thanks to Tom Boardman (his first publisher, with interests also in the film business), who had lent him professional scripts for guidance, considerable technical expertise to go with it by the time the real opportunities began to come his way.

He was taken up first by Anna Neagle and Herbert Wilcox to work on a series of films for the new singing sensation Frankie Vaughan, at three thousand pounds a script (which in today's money would be about twenty times that). This must have brought a big change in Jack's lifestyle - away from his two homes, at any rate - although he tends rather to deny it. But he was travelling down to London now not to work in the airless offices of the pulp industry for Mr Emmanuel, but to spend the day in Anna Neagle's penthouse on Park Lane, breaking off work to take refreshment amongst the celebrities of the film world in *Les Ambassadeurs* and other exclusive establishments. He bought a stylish Armstrong Siddeley coupé and sometimes drove Anna Neagle around London, once through sheer nervousness going the wrong way around Marble Arch. In spite of their glamorous image, he remembers them as quite ordinary, approachable people - she used to ask him to bring to the penthouse quantities of soil for indoor plant potting, which he had to carry over long distances sometimes. To get to know Frankie Vaughan he was sent up to Liverpool for an expenses-paid fortnight. One day they came upon a pair of feet sticking out from under a car in a country lane which belonged to the young Ken Dodd, they discovered. Frankie Vaughan (in a letter) remembers Jack's kindness to him at a desperately important time in his own career. The first film was *These Dangerous Years* (released in 1957), with Frankie playing a teenage gang-leader who reforms. The singer even then was doing work on behalf of boys' clubs, and it was in connection with this work that a Royal Premiere was staged (though with only second-division royals in attendance), to which Jack was invited. He of course arrived late (this was the occasion when he diverted his driver Bill Johnson to Evelyn's house to deliver eggs). He found himself unable to pass the rope keeping back the fans and became trapped in a corner, where a photographer, taking him for some kind of assistant, proceeded to aim spent flash bulbs in his direction that were too hot to handle. One film in the series, *The Heart of a Man*, gave Frankie Vaughan one of his biggest early song hits.

In 1957 there was a visit to the Cannes Film Festival, and for this Jack took along his schoolteacher girlfriend, who was still a lodger in Meynell Cottage. Two couchettes were booked for the rail trip through France, though in the event of course only one was used. The plan went beautifully, his girlfriend returning home separately, having supposedly been on holiday elsewhere. Ross may have been just a little suspicious (she makes no mention of the episode in her book), but it happened that just then Jack's mother had been taken into hospital. He visited her there almost straight from the boat train. It was his first experience of terminal illness, and like many another he missed the warning signs, even when they were pointed out to him.

"You realise your mother is very ill, of course," the doctor said.

"Yes, I know," said Jack.

"I mean *very* ill."

But somehow on these occasions the true situation is never quite spelled out. And besides, Rhoda had told him that she had been up in the night rummaging in the kitchens for something to eat for a bed-ridden fellow patient. Reassured, he went home in spite of the doctor's remarks. Very soon afterwards, however, came the devastating news that his mother had died. It was the only occasion he can remember in their years together when he was spontaneously hugged by Ross.

Jack was sent to Gibraltar, ostensibly for a holiday, though with a strong nudge that if he should happen to pick up a good story in which Frankie could be a fisherman with a jaunty hat, that would be fine. The result was a script that became *Wonderful Things*. He returned home this time - his girlfriend still in residence - to find that the French railways had reimbursed him for the cost of the unused couchette during the Cannes trip - a fantastic development, bearing in mind that no claim had ever been made. Ross had also taken up the habit of intercepting interesting mail, and the returned money was enough to alert her to the deception, or at any rate to confirm it. Jack's schoolteacher had to pack her bags. It wasn't the end of their romance, however; in fact it became easier for them to spend time together once she had moved to new lodgings. But of course the rent was lost.

Working on the Frankie Vaughan films - even though they are scarcely milestones in cinema history - was one of Story's most satisfying periods as a scriptwriter: he liked the people, worked on the scripts alone, was given quite a free hand, and the films were all actually made. From then on, although he continued to earn big money, scriptwriting became a more frustrating business. He was paid, for instance, four thousand pounds by Twentieth Century Fox for his work on "The White Rabbit", the wartime story of Wing Commander Yeo Thomas, an SOE spy who was the only man to escape from Buchenwald prison camp (in a coffin). That film was never actually made for cinema, although it became a TV film later on, having by then passed through the hands of other scriptwriters. And he was well paid by Renown Pictures for "Victorian County", a Jack Trevor Story original idea built around what would nowadays be called a theme park. That too was never made. Next he worked for Jay Lewis, an autocratic, free-swearing producer/director whose wealth and influence derived from his corny but hugely successful mid-fifties comedy *The Baby and the Battleship*. Lewis put him to work on "Hearts and Flowers", which was to star Rex Harrison and Sophia Loren, who would meet at a graveside, each having killed a long line of spouses, and themselves marry, to spend the rest of the picture trying to bump off one another. Lewis liked to be very close to the writing of the script, and would sometimes simply use his writer almost as a typist. Jack spent months at Jay Lewis's home in Chipperfield, a popular village with film people, where Peter Sellers was evidently the local "squire"; but eventually the project folded because Sophia Loren had meanwhile become inconveniently pregnant. That was what Jack was told, at any rate; you could never tell how true or complete the given information on a film project was. They were properties, and as such passed from producer to producer - and hence writer to writer - in strictly business deals. If it suited the owner of a property, the new scriptwriter would not be told who had worked on the film before him, nor even where the story idea had come from. "Hearts and Flowers", for instance, was based on a West End stage play, although Jack only discovered that later. Such practices lead to confusion in the memories of old hands in the game, who might believe they were responsible for a certain script, under a certain director, when the credits for the final version went to others. Story wrote *Modesty Blaise*, for example, but then so did a good many other writers.

These minor British of European film moguls could be as eccentric in their various ways, and as baffling in their origins, as their more illustrious counterparts in Hollywood. Where possible they used their power ruthlessly; money was everything. In appearance (according to Jack), Jay Lewis was a gnome-like version of Rex Harrison. He spoke with the same accent, too, but more gruffly, and with the word "fucking" inserted wherever it could be fitted. He used an old-fashioned megaphone, through which he would bark his commands to his players and crew. "I love to swear at fucking actors, Jack," he used to say. "Especially when there are people from the fucking film magazines around." But Lewis had climbed the greasy pole in the film business by taking a job as a chauffeur so as to get to know the influential people who could help him in his ascent. One day a load of film he was carrying caught fire and went up like a bomb. The resulting notoriety (so he once told Jack) projected him into an assistant director's job.

On the face of it the producers and directors were in the happiest position, with the writers as their slaves. But their lives were dominated by money worries - waiting interminably for deals to be concluded, contracts to be signed. The scriptwriter, once the job was finished, could take the money and move on. Jack Trevor Story was something of a special case, though. The Hitchcock film had made him a bankable asset when producers were trying to raise money. They would take him along to meetings with the money men as walking proof that their pet project was a sure winner.

In a biography as compressed as this - and Jack Trevor Story's could run potentially to as many volumes as Sir Winston Churchill's - it isn't possible to mention every girl in his life (he always talks about girls rather than women). He would be hard pressed himself to remember them all, anyway. One he appears to have forgotten but who crops up in Ross's book should be mentioned because she was a catalyst in the move to Worthing in 1960.

Ross does acknowledge that there was an improvement in their financial state once Jack had broken into the more lucrative film work. He proposed a holiday for his second family in Littlehampton. There was a problem, however, in as much as Ross was addicted to pets - always had been. Wherever she lived she soon had a houseful of cats, plus maybe a dog, and other smaller animals, too. (A figure of thirty-five cats has been mentioned in relation to one house; each had its own name and special call.) The livestock couldn't be left unattended; but Jack had a ready solution. A secretary he knew in television had said she wanted to get away from London for a week's holiday. The girl also happened to be fond of animals, so where better to spend this break than in the cottage in Harpenden while the family were away at the seaside? She struck Ross as rather plain, and she looked to be in her thirties, too. Jack's taste was for much younger females, so there seemed little reason - except that a stay in Harpenden seemed an odd way of getting away from London - to suspect that the proposal was not genuine. In her gullible way, Ross consented. Jack did travel down to Littlehampton with them, but on Monday he remembered an appointment with the studio, and the urgent need to revise certain scripts at home. Ross and the children were left to enjoy Littlehampton as best they could. The town had few attractions, especially for children, and was dirty, too. They were soon tired of it. When Jack came back mid-week she asked to be taken home. He resisted this for a few days, insisting that he needed a rest. They returned to Meynell Cottage at the weekend, obliging the girl, who had looked after the cats competently enough, to leave a little sooner than planned. She seemed pretty anxious to get away in any case.

Immediately after this unhappy holiday break Lee became ill with symptoms of polio, having recently been immunised, a procedure then in its infancy. A desperately anxious time followed for both parents, with Jack at one stage having to dash with a sample of spinal fluid to another hospital for analysis to speed up the diagnosis, which confirmed polio. They thought the boy might have contracted the disease from the immunisation, though the final medical verdict was that the vaccine had probably saved his life, or at any rate saved him from severe paralysis. In the event he was only mildly affected and even that cleared up by itself. Lee's was the only case in the whole of Hertfordshire; Ross blamed it on the dirty beach at Littlehampton.

Some months afterwards she came upon a postcard from the television girl to Jack which was incriminating enough to alert her to what had happened during their holiday treat. Ross was suddenly sick of his affairs, and of Meynell Cottage itself, which she had hated from the start. Thinking of moving down to the South Coast - and in terms of a separation - she put the property on the market without consultation and immediately found a buyer (Mr Simpson seemingly no longer having a claim on the garden shed). But to her surprise, Jack said he wanted them to stay together. He even talked of yet another fresh start.

Littlehampton notwithstanding, Ross was fond of the South Coast, which she associated with happy childhood holidays. She took to Worthing instantly. They bought a red-brick three-story terraced house on York Road and moved in with about eight cats. Lorel was now pretty well off her hands and she was writing again. Her autobiography in this period is mainly concerned with domestic matters, however, in which Jack figures very little.

He, by contrast, loathed Worthing, if a piece in *Letters to an Intimate Stranger* is a true guide. He talks of the "stink of the seaweed", while she describes its odour as a "blessing". But what upset him most were all the pensioners - you could find nobody to talk to under seventy-five. It was like suddenly discovering you're in the wrong queue and it's for the graveyard. Eventually he found a coffee bar on the front where the few young people in the town congregated (he was past forty himself by now), and this led to minor adventures. But he wouldn't have spent much time in Worthing in any case. His scriptwriting always took him away from home for long periods, and of course there was Evelyn and his other family to visit in Welwyn Garden City. Sometimes he worked there, too, if it happened to be convenient.

A novel from this period merits a mention; *Man Pinches Bottom*. In fact there is no telling when the book was written, or where. It may even have been a re-vamped Sexton Blake. Percy Paynter is a commercial artist drawing comic characters for Consolidated Periodicals, an old-fashioned organisation sheltering an extraordinary range of minor publications and now threatened with takeover by the "Reflection" newspaper, which has streamlining plans. (This battle was based on the real fifties takeover of Amalgamated Press by the *Daily Mirror* group; the Sexton Blake Library, saved by Bill Baker, was a near casualty.) Already unsettled, Paynter makes the mistake of pinching the wrong bottom in the lift one morning, and is sacked. Confident of being able to go it alone as a freelance, he also has an opportunity now to adopt the more bohemian lifestyle he hankers for. But as a result of a number of minor happenings, and a jumping to unfounded conclusions by the Reflection's star reporter Mike "Crusader" Farrago, he is suddenly on the front pages as a suspected child molester and kidnapper. His comic creations are bizarrely interpreted as evidence of a sick mind. Immersed in his new lifestyle, however, Paynter hasn't seen the papers. Emerging innocently from hiding one day, he is set upon by an army of hysterical mothers and almost killed. *Man Pinches Bottom* is a more accomplished piece of work than *The Money Goes Round and Round* (which in truth is something of a one-joke book), and one of Story's own favourites. It has several times come close to being filmed.

Also from this same period is *Mix Me a Person*, in which Sexton Blake becomes a lady psychiatrist. A crime story set in the coffee-bar era of the late fifties, it gave Adam Faith his first starring role in films.

Jay Lewis, meanwhile, had put Jack to work on two films which were to star Spike Milligan. The first was *Postman's Knock*, an idea settled on by Lewis by the procedure of eliminating workaday jobs until he reached one that hadn't been done. An innocent village postman comes to work in the big city and finds himself accidentally mixed up in criminal activity. He catches the crooks and becomes a hero. Story reckons the second film was better, *Invasion Quartet*, based on a Norman Collins story, in which four boffins set about silencing a Nazi gun trained on Dover; but it sounds an odd subject for farce and a curious vehicle for Spike Milligan, whose work on the "Goon Show" was just ending.

Jack's more vivid memories are of Milligan himself, in action at the MGM studios. One day he arrived with a long tale of how that morning he had had to cook breakfast for his family because his wife had run off with someone, then dodged people waiting outside from the Inland Revenue who were trying to serve a court order on him. "Am I a film star or not?" Spike asked his canteen audience. Then he drew from his pocket that day's delivery of bills, final demands and summonses and proceeded to sing the contents.

Sometimes they used to play the guitar together, and once Spike called Jack a "shit" when he declined an invitation for drinks with the excuse that he had to collect his wife from her cleaning job at ICI in Welwyn. That was Evelyn, and at the time he was supposed to be living with Ross in Worthing. In the same MGM canteen Jack recalls opening a door for Vivien Leigh, who gave him a nice smile (she was working on *The Roman Spring of Mrs Stone* with Warren Beatty); and equally memorably, seeing George Sanders sitting alone and tucking into egg and chips. (None of which is intended to suggest that Jack Trevor Story dwells on his past encounters with celebrities. He doesn't.)

The phrase "live now, pay later" so aptly sums up both the late fifties on-the-never-never culture and Jack Trevor Story's spontaneous approach to life, complete with consequences, that it might be thought to have originated with his famous novel and the associated film. Not so; it was in common usage long before then. Nor did Story pluck it from the air. His own title for the novel was "Jam Tomorrow". "Live Now, Pay Later" was suggested by the actor Laurence Harvey, who was briefly engaged by Jay Lewis, at tremendous potential expense, to star in the film. But Harvey was linked to American money, which at some point was cut off. That left the film without a star, but with a perfect title.

Lewis had first asked Story to adapt a novel by someone else - a tale of a housewife who gets herself into debt and goes on the streets rather than confess to her husband. He turned the job down (this would be just after his long stint on the Spike Milligan films), but then the tally-boy activities of his friend Bill Johnson gave him the idea for a book on the never-never theme of his own. He wrote it in nine days and took the manuscript by prior agreement to Jay Lewis, who sat down and read it while Jack hung around in the same room.

"You've gone through a door, old boy!" was Lewis's instant reaction. Jack had moved on from the comedy thrillers he had been writing into true social comedy and indeed social realism.

But his publishers W H Allen were unimpressed. Editor Jeffrey Simmons told him that he would always have a cult following but would never be a real commercial proposition. Jack next went to Secker & Warburg, who with a film now in prospect took the book on. A Penguin paperback followed.

Story had certainly gone through a door in terms of his literary reputation, but not as it transpired financially. Jeffrey Simmons was at least half right. Despite terrific reviews and the boost to sales of a successful film, *Live Now, Pay Later* was never a best-seller. It sold out the first edition of a few thousand copies, but didn't go much beyond that, scarcely earning back for the publishers the author's advance. Many more copies were of course sold in the Penguin edition (he remembers a figure of eighty-five thousand), but Story benefited very little from that since hardback publishers always stitched up paperback royalties so as to ensure they wouldn't be out of pocket.

As to the film, Story went bankrupt over it. For a total fee of three thousand pounds - and the money would only trickle through in meagre instalments - Jay Lewis had him working on the script for a year, during which time it was re-written nine times. "I never know what I like until I see it," Lewis would say as script succeeded script. But in fact he was slowly taking the heart out of the film and replacing it with jokes and comic situations straight out of *The Baby and the Battleship*. It was a process analogous to Evelyn Waugh's short story "Excursion in

Reality", in which an author is put to work on a modern and increasingly bizarre version of Shakespeare, only to have the producer finally shake his head over the resulting travesty and demand a turn to the purity of the original. Lewis called in despair for Jack's original novel, still then in manuscript, and declared they would proceed on the basis of that without further meddling. Meanwhile Story had run into debt and had to borrow from the bank to stay afloat. Further debts piled up so that when the long-awaited "end money" at last came through it was quickly claimed by his creditors.

But the film was well received, Ian Hendry, mesmeric in the Bill Johnson inspired part of Albert Argyle, attracting most praise. Ross had actually suggested Hendry to Jack, who passed the idea on to the studio; she had been impressed by his performance in a television play. There was a special screening in London in 1989 to coincide with the publication of a new edition of the novel in that year by Allison & Busby. The book has probably lasted better - a classic of its day which can certainly be placed on a par with *Room at the Top*, *Saturday Night and Sunday Morning*, *Billy Liar* and *A Kind of Loving*, even if they all (I would guess) outsold it.

It is impossible to say what happened to the money Story earned *before Live Now, Pay Later*. Of course there were families and houses and cars and living expenses, but we are talking about many thousands of pounds. It didn't all go to the tax man, certainly. Whereas nowadays, with only a small income from writing, he is careful to keep precise accounts; back then, when the money was flowing in, he made no such effort. His financial affairs, once the crunch came, could only be explored and assessed in sit-down interviews with the official receiver, longer and more detailed than the ones I've conducted for the writing of this book. Besides films, he had earnings from journalism (he wrote at one time or another for just about every magazine or newspaper you can think of), and television (he has counted a total of seventy-three scripts that were actually screened, mainly in the fifties and sixties, from original plays to individual episodes of established series); but the fees were only counted at best in hundreds, and of course such sums could run through his fingers in a very short time. Film money was what he really needed, but films by the early sixties were losing out to television, with cinemas all over the country starting to close down or convert to bingo halls. Scripting work was becoming harder to find. Jay Lewis had gone quiet, but fortunately there was another important director in Story's life, Mario Zampi.

Their association had begun when Mario Zampi took Herbert Wilcox to court (or threatened to) over the Frankie Vaughan film *Wonderful Things*, which Jack had written in Gibraltar. Zampi claimed that the story had been stolen from one of his own films. In both, it seems, a poor Spanish fisherman forsakes his childhood sweetheart for a white Anglo-Saxon millionairess - something like that. There was no truth in the allegation, but Mario Zampi had to be appeased to the tune of ten thousand pounds to prevent *Wonderful Things* being blocked. Jack looked to be in hot water, despite his innocence; but all that came out of the affair so far as he was concerned was an approach from Mario Zampi, who expressed an interest in using him as a scriptwriter. Between producers, ten thousand pounds was a trivial sum.

Mario Zampi was at least as important a figure in Jack Trevor Story's life and career as either Jay Lewis or the Herbert Wilcox - Anna Neagle team. He is harder to write about with any clarity, however, because none of the films on which they worked together was ever made. Jack describes him as a very glamorous character. He made him a member of the Rheingold Club and opened up opportunities for him to wine and dine the current crop of film starlets, top models and such. This was actually a kind of work; its purpose was to allow the scriptwriter time to impress on a particular starlet the role and character which she might be expected to play. Of course the scriptwriter might begin to develop other ideas, too, as the evening wore on. Invariably, though, the starlet would be accompanied, however discreetly, by her hired bruiser. Story in any case doesn't seem to have been especially attracted to the idea of short-time sessions with girls in the film business. At heart he was still a romantic, and this inclined him to try to court them - to the amazement, naturally, of the producers. More ordinary girls seem to have appealed to him more, and one day early in 1963, travelling by train from Worthing up to London and Mario Zampi's sumptuous office in Wardour Street, he met and fell for another. I will call her Eunice.

One of the things that seems to puzzle Jack Trevor Story retrospectively is that (with the late exception of Elaine Hepple) all of the significant women in his life have been, as he puts it, straight - that is to say conventionally minded. As a general rule he can't abide straight people. Why, therefore, did he always seem to settle on straight women?

One reason might be that there weren't so many *unconventionally* minded women around: a man with a mind as unusual as Jack Trevor Story's could spend several lifetimes searching for one true soul mate. But another explanation is that he never really did the chasing. True, he had a roving eye, a ready tongue and the capacity to charm the birds off the trees; but the women he has "clicked" with always met him at least half way, and more often some distance beyond that point. *They* wanted *him*. So far as he was concerned they could have been anybody, just so long as they were female, moderately good-looking, and available.

How else to explain the sudden presence in his complicated life of this new girl from Finchley, Eunice, a twenty-two year old blonde total stranger, met casually on a train? She had no great interest in books or writing as such, and came from a perfectly conventional, admirably straight, family background. Jack found her attractive and likeable - he describes her as a very witty girl - but she was hardly a soul mate. The reason for his initial approach - she was sitting alone in an empty restaurant car - is obvious enough, his romantic nature notwithstanding. After that the push towards a more serious relationship probably came most strongly from her.

Jack discounts the attraction to women of his show-business and media links, but it happens that he was carrying with him on the train that day his new novel, *Live Now, Pay Later*, together with an impressive review from one of the Sunday papers. He surely wasn't keeping them out of sight, and he was on his way, too, to a meeting with a famous producer to discuss a projected film sequel, *Something for Nothing*. Eunice, he insists, would have been quite unimpressed by all this. Really? is all one can say. She was an ordinary girl, leading an ordinary life - in fact she told Jack that she had just spent a boring week at the Butlin's hotel in Brighton. A different world must have beckoned as Jack chatted modestly about his novel-writing, film and television activities. She was willing at any rate to hurry down to London to dine with him later at the Studio Club in Piccadilly. Afterwards Jack abandoned his plan to take a taxi back to Worthing (and there's a glimpse of where some of the money was going), and they spent the night together in a nearby hotel.

Poor Eunice had no idea then what kind of life she would be leading as Jack Trevor Story's mistress. He installed her in a flat in Goring, just along the front from Worthing, and one of the first things she did was to buy a dog for company, since he had to be away so much. The dog was a tiny, hand-sized poodle puppy, which would later become famous in his *Guardian* column (and inspire his superb novel *Little Dog's Day*). It was supposed to be a guard-dog, but at first was so small and timid that it couldn't jump off the edge of the carpet.

Meanwhile - and unknown to Eunice - temporarily flush with a big advance from Mario Zampi for *Something for Nothing* (in which Albert Argyle progresses from foot-in-the-door peddling of the wares of Callendar's Warehouse to bored housewives into the more political trading-stamps game), Ross and Jack had been house-hunting again. They had bought a large and impressive house in its own grounds (it had a drive all the way around) on Arundel Road, in an outlying part of Worthing. It was exactly the kind of place he had always wanted - perfect for entertaining his friends and contacts in the film and publishing worlds. It had a conservatory, which Ross immediately had converted into a spacious study for Jack, all done out in formica, then a new and tasteful material. Sadly, he never really moved in. He tried to, but the telephone never stopped ringing. Often it was Eunice, at first to chat, but later, as his domestic situation became clearer to her, to demand when he was going to leave his wife or wives and move in more permanently with her. Whatever he may have told her, he probably had no such specific plan. He was always genuinely and painfully torn between his domestic and love commitments, and driven to try to hold things together on all fronts. But then Eunice, too, became pregnant - and at just the moment when the money was drying up and they were about to be evicted from the Goring flat.

Ross already had suspicions, from the phone calls, that Jack had yet another new girl; she received confirmation of the fact from an unexpected source - Evelyn. The two had remained friends through the years, and even though it had been part of Ross's plan in moving to Worthing to try to separate the children so as to allow them to develop independently, contacts and visits had continued. One day Evelyn took the younger children for a trip down to Worthing. While she was occupied in buying ice-cream on the front, Caroline turned and saw her dad go by in his big Jaguar (which had now replaced the Armstrong Siddeley) with a blonde and a dog in the passenger seat."Mum, mum," she cried excitedly, "I've just seen dad! . ."

But no sooner had Ross found out about Eunice than Jack brought the girl home. She was in much the same position as Ross herself had been in back in the forties when presented to Evelyn: pregnant and homeless. And Jack put to her the same question he had put to Evelyn long ago. Even more amazing, the possibility of Eunice moving in with them was actually discussed. Ross always had an airing cupboard full of kittens, and on the pretext of seeing them she invited the girl upstairs for a private chat. But it didn't work out. Both women came down again in tears, and Jack had to think about making other arrangements. It would mean having to give up the pretence that the lovely big house on Arundel Road was his home - a painful adjustment for him.

Jack and Eunice effectively went on the road. He couldn't take her home, pregnant, to her conventional parents in Finchley; nor could he abandon her. They slept in country hotels they couldn't afford until the money was all but gone and at last threw themselves on the mercy of Jack's half-brother, Bernard, who at that time was managing the Station Hotel in Cambridge. He put them in a tiny attic room. There were no cooking facilities; they had to prepare meals using a cheap frying-pan from Woolworths over a small electric fire turned on its back. Fortunately a nephew (one of Elsa's sons) had a greengrocer's shop in Chesterton, from where they were able to scrounge a little food and money. Mario Zampi meanwhile was telephoning frantically all over about the neglected script. Jack had been sending in odd bits when he could, but he was really needed in Wardour Street. Some money must have come through, for they were able at length to move into a cottage close to Duxford airfield. But then one day he phoned the office and was dumbfounded to hear that Mario Zampi had died the previous day. It meant that *Something for Nothing* would never be filmed now - that for the present at least all film scripting work was at an end - but Jack remembers chiefly felling terribly guilty when he was told the news. Mario had been a good friend to him and he had let him down. Before long he would remember the glamorous film producer in one of his very best novels, *I Sit in Hanger Lane*.

Eunice couldn't go through with having the baby, so the necessary arrangements had to be made - at a cost of three hundred pounds, divided between a psychiatrist, doctor and nursing home. It established an unfortunate pattern; more terminations would follow in the years they were together. The girl Treasure in the Albert Argyle novels goes through the same thing, with more tragic (if fictional) consequences in her case. Strangely, though, the fictional terminations preceded the real-life ones - must have done since Jack had already written *Something for Nothing* when he and Eunice first met.

Eunice was a camera lady (she was also an accomplished photographer who had her work published in the magazines) and Jack was able to find her a job in Cambridge while they were living in the Duxford cottage. This also was the beginning of a pattern, in as much as he would tend as the years passed to live increasingly off the modest earnings of his women. But however erratic his own earnings, he was never idle. In the cottage, in three weeks, he wrote the third book in the trilogy, *The Urban District Lover,* in which Albert becomes his own boss. In this final novel, foolishly perhaps, the character is killed off - an eventuality announced in the very first sentence. The writing, he remembers, coincided with the Earls Court Ideal Homes Exhibition in London, for it was there that he met Ross and the kids for a final family conference, which they held in a Danish show-house with interested spectators looking in through the windows. Secker & Warburg responded with an immediate payment of one thousand pounds for *The Urban District Lover,* yet Jack and Eunice continued somehow to live in the most dire poverty. Each Saturday morning he had to wire ten pounds to Evelyn and ten pounds to Ross, and often there would be nothing left. So anxious was he about Ross's state of mind that sometimes they would drive in the big Jag (which he was managing to keep) all the way down to Worthing, simply to sit outside the house, looking for signs that she and the children were all right. He was crying, Eunice was crying, and inside Ross would doubtless be crying, too. It was a terribly unhappy time for everyone (except possibly for Evelyn, who was well used to all this). Eunice once told him that he cried whenever he saw school kids pass the cottage window. She had the feeling, of course, that he wanted to go back to his family.

But a change of mood, and even in a minor way of fortune, did come. He remembers one night as they were doing their long circuit of the airfield with the dog he saw a satellite moving almost imperceptibly across the sky. He read it not as a portent, but as a sign of better times ahead. And next morning he saw a dead bird in the gutter - not a discovery to cheer up most people, but birds had appeared at turning points in his life before (and would do so again). This bird's message was that if there was life there must be hope. He returned to the cottage strangely uplifted and almost immediately was telephoned by Louis Marks, a producer at Rediffusion, who invited him to submit storylines for episodes of the police series *No Hiding Place*. He had already done *Escaper's Club* (based on Colditz) for Rediffusion; this new approach would lead to a great deal more television work for both channels.

No immediate pay day was in sight, however; they fell into rent arrears and were kicked out of their Duxford home. Eunice went back to her parents for a spell while Jack searched for somewhere else for them to live. In the same woods on the edge of Welwyn where he had conceived and set *The Trouble with Harry*, close to the Great North Road, he came by chance upon a caravan site inhabited by an oddball collection of writers, artists, musicians, gypsies and criminals, and presided over by an obese American ex-comedian in a cowboy hat, who reminded him a little of Sam Foster way back in Burwell. It seemed just the place.

Chapter Nine

MAGGIE ON SATURDAY

Fond of and attached to him as Jack Trevor Story's girlfriends used to be, a feature of the relationships was that each had from the start a kind of get-out clause. Maggie, later, would always say she wanted to live in Paris. Later still, Elaine would have in mind a course of study at university. As for the girl I have called Eunice, she dreamed aloud of one day moving to Jersey.

The caravan life was enjoyable, but primitive. The little community was decidedly colourful, with impromptu jazz band sessions apt to be interrupted by the sudden arrival of police cars looking for stolen loot. (Nowadays it would be drugs.) Amongst the musicians were clarinetist Monty Sunshine (who would soon have his own successful band on the strength of his hit record *"Petit Fleur"*), base-player Tony Bagot and trumpeter Rod Mason. Eunice fitted easily enough into that side of the life, but the more primitive aspects were harder to take. Winter in the caravan was desperate, with minimal heating and regularly frozen water pipes. One cold day Bill Johnson (who turned up everywhere) arrived to find Jack under the caravan dressed in little more than pyjamas, trying to warm up the pipes with a candle. Each morning, too, there was the slopping out, a ritual much complained about in *prison* life. Eunice had taken a job as a hospital receptionist, for which she had to arrive punctually and presentably. She seldom, therefore, spent the night in the caravan, preferring to sleep at home in Finchley. They were still together as a couple, but the relationship was in decline. Jack has said many times in interviews and print that sex for him lasts for about three weeks, after which he begins to lose interest. He and Eunice had by now been together for about three years. But the sex apart, it was an exhausting and humiliating life for a conventionally minded and inexperienced young woman. She used to complain that she felt as if she had a steel band around her head that was growing ever tighter. The pressure was becoming unbearable.

And they even got kicked out of the caravan. The fat cowboy comedian, whose relaxed regime had allowed Jack to sink into his customary rent arrears, was replaced by a far meaner landlord who wouldn't tolerate debt, especially if the debtor happened to be a writer. They were given two weeks to find yet another new place.

Or rather Jack was. By now he was virtually on his own. He remembers a tiring day driving the big Jag around all the estate agents in the north London area looking for an inexpensive flat. By late afternoon he had become lost and decided to get back to the caravan before nightfall. But then he saw one last office. Dropping with fatigue, he tried there. The woman sat him down and made him a cup of tea, but as with all the previous estate agents there seemed to be nothing available. There was only one possibility, a room in a shared flat overlooking Hampstead Heath. It had been given nominally to someone else, but if he could put down a deposit ahead of his rival he could have it. By some miracle, Jack had money in his pocket that day. The room was his. He would find himself living improbably next door to the Burtons (Richard and Elizabeth), with other celebrities as near neighbours. He hadn't even known he was in Hampstead.

Eunice helped him to move in, then she at last threw away the steel band and headed for Jersey, as she had always wanted to do. She had a friend there, and employment prospects. She came back to Hampstead for a few visits, but their life together was over. Of his important girlfriends, she is the only one to have remained in (occasional) touch.

Jack felt lonelier with her departure than he had expected. He was in no mood, however, to return on any sort of living-in basis to either of his families. On an impulse he travelled one day to Butlin's holiday camp at Clacton, picturing it as being full of free-living teenage girls. As always when on the road in this period, he had with him his guitar, his typewriter, and Eunice's abandoned poodle, which she had called Beauty. Arriving thus encumbered at the reception desk, he was told that the guitar and typewriter were okay, but not the dog. Butlin's holiday camps did not allow dog visitors.

"Oh shit!" said Jack, a phrase he had used so many times before at frustrating moments in his up-and-down-life.

He drove around and happened to notice a procession of young girls entering a hotel.

"That's the place for us," he told the dog.

They checked in, but Jack was pregnant with another novel and decided to leave the teenage beauties till next morning. He had a preference anyway for daytime chatting up because the motive would appear more innocent. Next day, however, he discovered that the girls had vanished like a mirage.

"Where did they all go?" he asked the receptionist, herself quite a comely lady, not yet in middle-age.

"Oh, we had a dance on," she explained.

"I see," said Jack. "Ah well, at least I managed to make a start on my new novel last night."

"Did you really?" said the receptionist, with genuine interest.

She was Rita, from somewhere like Ipswich, a youngish widow whose husband, it transpired, had died suddenly at breakfast between boiled eggs, like Scott Fitzgerald. They spent much of that summer together (1967). She was a marvellous lover (Jack uses another word), but she lived in a fussy little bungalow with wall-to-wall carpeting, and Jack can't stand wall-to-wall people, as he calls them (they nowadays comprise just about everybody). Soon she was linking him threateningly when they were out walking together and beginning to talk about the furnishings *they* would have. Next thing she too was pregnant.

This pregnancy unfortunately coincided with Jack's latest and most spectacular bankruptcy. For ages he had been ignoring demands from his bank and the inland revenue, and one or the other finally took him to court. His debts were estimated at around seven thousand pounds, which even allowing for inflation seems a smallish sum. But *Live Now, Pay Later* was still quite recent (his earlier bankruptcy, if such it was in the precise legal sense, had preceded the film), and the living out of the theme by its very author proved irresistible to the papers, quality and tabloid alike. The bankruptcy was reported on page one of the *Times* and page three of the *Sun*, and everywhere else besides, with photographs, the new bankrupt looking suitably disreputable.

Poor Rita nearly died. From somewhere the three hundred pounds needed to square matters with her was produced. On a visit to the nursing home, to his hidden relief, Jack was told that she didn't want to see him *ever again*. But it had been a wonderful summer.

As to the novel he had begun in preference to chatting up the teenage girls on that first evening in Rita's hotel, Jack thinks it may have been *Little Dog's Day*, though he can't be sure. Certainly it wasn't *I Sit in Hanger Lane*, his first published novel after the Albert books. That had been written during the caravan period. What distinguishes Jack Trevor Story from his contemporaries (if not most writers from all periods) is that whereas they, having established their name and a certain style, have rather tended to keep on writing what amounts to the same book; he has continued to develop. It is his chief claim, I would suggest, to serious consideration - and recognition - as one of the best British writers of the late twentieth century; but it explains also, I think, why his books have had quite a narrow appeal, and why he has steadily lost readers. With *I Sit in Hanger Lane* he went through another door (in Jay Lewis's phrase). The book was his first venture into first-person writing, and his most autobiographical to date. Sometimes he argues that Jack Trevor Story is a very different, altogether more civilised creature from the scriptwriter Horace Spurgeon Fenton, *Hanger Lane's* narrator; but the similarities are strong. Detectable for the first time, too, in this book is a readiness to put off the kind of reader he felt he had outgrown. Horace is first seen living with a girl in quite appalling conditions on a caravan site, much as Jack and Eunice were doing at the time. She didn't want to be recognisable in the book, however, so she had to be disguised. He decided to make Horace's fictional girl a cripple - left alone all day and then carried in the nick of time to a wretched outdoor loo. But there is something fishy about this crippled girl's condition (how she has come to be in his life is only explained much later.) Is she paraplegic? Evidently not, for she has excellent control of her bladder. Also, she can support herself for a moment at the door of the loo while Horace cleans the seat, and control her feet sufficiently to avoid the puddles of urine. Again, normal sex would appear to be possible, even though people are speculating otherwise. It is all very unpleasant, and the fishiness adds to the unpleasantness. This book would not appeal to the prurient; in fact one can imagine casual readers of all kinds would find it hard to turn the first pages - just, one fancies, as the author intended.

But before I begin to put off readers of the right as well as the wrong sort, let me swiftly quote Michael Moorcock, in his prefatory note to the recently published (as I write) new Allison & Busby edition:

> Treasure it. It's one of the funniest, most humane, most truthful books published anywhere for a long time.

The novel had its admirers while still in typescript, one of whom was Peter Sellers. It told, probably for the first time, what the life of a moderately successful film scriptwriter could actually be like in the late fifties, early sixties period. Most people would probably have pictured someone like Noel Coward, with cigarette holder and smoking jacket. Dedicated "to the memory of a dead friend", *Hanger Lane* mixes Story's own wildly improvable love and domestic entanglements (Evelyn becomes Edna; Ross, Tres) with the even crazier insanity of the film world. Mario Zampi (the "dead friend" of the dedication) is faithfully portrayed in the character of film producer Arturo Conti, his methods and mannerisms beautifully described in Chapter 10. As for Hanger Lane itself, it's a pre-M25 main west London thoroughfare in which Jack himself seemed always to be held up in traffic as he shuttled unceasingly - ding-dong, ding-dong - between his bewildering private and business lives and commitments.

I Sit in Hanger Lane would win high praise later, but his publishers of the Albert Argyle books, Secker & Warburg, at first refused it, just as W H Allen had rejected *Live Now, Pay Later*. His editor complained that the book contained all his worst writing - in essence it was too autobiographical; he pilloried himself too much. But soon afterwards Jack received a letter from Tom Warburg, a senior partner, asking him not to be disheartened by this one rejection; they were still interested in publishing him. In response, Jack took the opportunity to praise, in passing, a recently published volume by Warburg himself. Next, the firm called for the manuscript again, for a re-assessment. In the meantime Jack had fortuitously sold the book to a pair of American film producers as part of a two-film deal - remarkable for a novel not yet printed.

"You've made great improvements here, Story," his editor now said. "*Great* improvements." And the unaltered manuscript was accepted for publication without further comment. It came out (in 1968) to ecstatic reviews; so ecstatic in fact that Seckers ran a "rave-review" ad in the *Evening Standard*. Sales were unaffected, however; they stuck stubbornly at his usual first-edition print run of around three thousand. As to the film, that was still some considerable distance away from any thought of shooting.

The two producers were Bob Booker and George Foster - both successful in America in their different ways. Jack Trevor Story's offerings were brought to their attention as a result of his having changed agents. Something had gone wrong with the Bob Fenn (MCA) representation, and he had been taken up by Rae Ellison of the Dina Lom agency, who were good in both films and television. Producer interest in *Hanger Lane* may also have been stimulated by Peter Sellers: Jack Trevor Story was evidently one of his favourite writers (Sellers once crept up behind him in the MGM canteen and did a "Guess who?" clasping of hands over eyes). He wanted to play Horace and offered initially to do the role without "up-front" money because of his admiration for Jack's work.

Story's second offering - probably more exciting as a concept to the film people that *Hanger Lane* - was "Echo-2", which existed as a treatment rather than a novel. As a result of his abortive earlier work on "The White Rabbit", Jack had a headful of background material to do with wartime spies, special operations, places where captive Germans had been tortured to death by such as the Free French, similar places where agents had been trained in the art of silent murder and other valuable wartime skills, and so on. "Echo-2 was a useful vehicle for all this stuff. An enemy agent has been left stranded in England at the end of the war, with a plan and map in his head for blowing up strategic targets in and around London. He assimilates into British life and his wartime mission lies dormant; but then an incident many years later re-awakens it. Jack modelled this on a real-life incident once at the cinema with Ross, who wouldn't stand up for "The Queen". (Curiously, she objected, he says, to the *hairstyles* of the Royal Family rather than their royal status.) Jack, too, remained seated, and was promptly set upon by a bunch of Young Conservatives sitting in the row behind. His German spy suffers a similar experience, but the beating is more severe and re-awakens his wartime orders. He begins to blow up buildings in what seems now a random and terrifying way, since in the years that have passed their old uses have been forgotten and they have become harmless things like coffee bars and nursery schools.

On offer was sixty-four thousand dollar contract (if the films actually went through; otherwise the pay-off would be much less), and the prospect of working with the producers in America - initially New York - expenses paid. This had strong appeal for Jack, not least because he saw the chance of earning big money that might be kept out of the hands of his creditors. Plainly it was an opportunity to jump at. As a bankrupt he ought to have surrendered his passport, but no one had told him that, or at any rate insisted on it.

There was another compelling reason to go abroad, too; he was being pestered by a new girlfriend. She was a beautiful Scottish girl whom one of his sons had met on a camping holiday; she lived in a shared flat in north London. Jack had met her there and was attracted, but at the same time he was resolved not to become amorously entangled again for the present. Eunice was in fact still visiting occasionally from Jersey, and their love wasn't quite dead so far as he was concerned. But the new girl was persistent, and one night, after a row with her flatmates, she turned up on his doorstep with her suitcases. Her name was Maggie.

Christmastime (1967) was approaching again, but Jack seems by now to have given up attending family gatherings in the old way (his eldest daughter Jacqueline was now thirty). He planned to spend Christmas in New York. Currently he was living part of the time at the Thatched Barn at Borehamwood, a hotel much used by media folk which had an interesting recent history in as much as it had served as a training base for secret agents (so at any rate he had been told). The atmosphere (real or imagined) would be a stimulus to his work on "Echo-2" - that was the idea, together with a desire to get away from Hampstead for a bit.

But Maggie had followed him there. When it was time to leave for the States she accompanied him to Heathrow, together with Bill Johnson and his girlfriend. They saw him through passport control, hung around and waved as the plane climbed into the sky, then returned at a leisurely pace to the Thatched Barn, where Bill had some unfinished business. They found Jack in his room, asleep in bed. He had had a sudden attack of claustrophobia - brought on by the failure of the aircraft to move for some time after the doors had been closed - and had aborted the trip.

So he and Maggie spent a happy Christmas together, while Bob and George fretted about their missing scriptwriter in New York. After the holiday they enquired about crossings by sea, only to find that regular sailings by ocean liner were now a thing of the past; the next one would be in February. So it had to be by plane. This time he didn't turn back. Flying over Iceland, taking photographs through the window, he was tapped on the shoulder by Ernie Wise. He and Eric Morecambe were on their way to take America by storm - except that Eric was on a different plane. Like royalty, they always travelled that way, said Ernie.

The reason why Jack had to travel to America to work on the films was to be close to the producers for script conferences and such, when they could be fitted into their busy schedules. A scriptwriter working on new projects was seldom urgently needed; he simply had to follow the producers wherever their current work happened to take them. It was really a kind of free holiday.

The producers even provided him with girls to take to concerts and other events. He dragged them to jazz concerts, featuring his musical heroes from times past. Most memorably, against advice, he went to see and hear the great Duke Ellington band (survivors anyway) in the cathedral of St John the Divine in Harlem. Another girl took him to a pot party in Brooklyn; she told him casually that she had been kidnapped by gunmen the previous weekend. He was startled to overhear talk at a different party of a small island somewhere entirely given over to the hatching of a plot to assassinate President Johnson. But most of his time in New York was spent with an intelligent and independently employed girl (she appeared on TV) who nevertheless proved to be an extraordinarily costly companion - so costly in fact that Jack wondered at times if she had been planted. He knew it was common enough for money men in the film business to use devious, and even criminal ways to recover money that had supposedly been paid in good faith to their various hirelings. But Jack was happy enough to have money run through his fingers or otherwise escape from his possession, since he didn't know how much of it he would manage to keep when he got home. The important thing was to have a good time, and he was certainly doing that. Maggie, meanwhile, was phoning him across the Atlantic on her temp's wages, mainly to play favourite records, such as Louis Armstrong's *What a Wonderful World.* With everyone who would listen, he was discussing the relative merits of his new and old girlfriends, as if they were all characters in a hit soap opera.

The producers and entourage now moved down to Nassau, in the Bahamas, where Jack was booked into the best hotel. This alerted the local con-men and minor villains to the presence in their midst of a man of apparent wealth. Half-imagined adventures followed, in which he may have been kidnapped several times. Threatening situations resolved by large tips or other generous payments can be so classified. He was given a super hire-car, only to find it transformed next morning into an old wreck with doors held fastened by string. On a speedboat trip he was asked to take over the controls when the man at the wheel lost his nerve. ("What are those black things in the water?" Jack had asked. "Fish or rocks?") One night he broadcast on local radio from a nightclub - probably choosing his girlfriends as his subject, for he had everyone in Nassau, too, weighing the pros and cons and advising on the best choice. Most memorably, he met the long-serving editor of the *Nassau Tribune,* Sir Etienne Dupuch, a campaigning newspaperman who nevertheless according to Lord Beaverbrook had shown more vision and better understanding of the glories of the British Empire than most of the newspapers in Great Britain. Sir Etienne remembered the Duke of Windsor's governorship of the islands. He admired the Duke's speeches, while deploring their content.

Next it was back to New York, and from there a flight back to London. As Jack was leaving the hotel, Maggie phoned to ask when he would be home. "In about two weeks," he told her, while the receptionist, who had had to deal with many of these calls, eyed his luggage and looked at him with contempt. His plan in fact was only to touch London and to fly on to Rome, where he was now required to be in this chasing game.

On the flight from Heathrow this time was Tony Hancock, bound for Australia and suicide. They exchanged no words, but Hancock did laugh, in his sardonic way, when the bottom fell out of a plastic bag Jack was carrying containing all of his clothes. The accident gave him something else to think about besides being locked up inside a stationary aeroplane. In Rome he booked into the Hassler, near the Spanish Steps, then immediately began to scan the papers for a flat and anything else of interest that might be going. In the *Daily American* a Greek lady taxi driver was advertising her services: she would take you shopping and promised to be very familiar. He telephoned and found she spoke unexpectedly good English. She seemed excited to hear from an English writer working in the movies. She found him an expensive but jerry-built apartment in the Monte Mario district and showed him the sights. Then she disappeared for a day or two, promising to return with something interesting. Jack tried a nightclub and soon found himself with a new female companion, a minor American show-biz journalist, who was interested in sharing his apartment. She seemed unwell, but he was happy to oblige her, nevertheless. Once installed, she told him she was pregnant by a Mafia man who wouldn't give her any money - would Jack phone a certain number and explain her plight to the man? She then took to her - or *his* - bed, sick and evidently growing sicker. Fortunately no one responded to his nervous attempt to contact her lover (language must have been a problem). He did manage to persuade a doctor to look in; he diagnosed pleurisy as well as pregnancy. When the Greek taxi driver lady returned she was very angry at his naiveté in getting himself entangled with an unknown sick woman with dangerous connections. But she had demands of her own to make. In her arms she was carrying an untidy, bulky manuscript. This was the reason why she had been so excited to meet an English writer. Once she had been notorious in England as the star of a breach-of-promise case against a prominent army officer. The press had dubbed her "The Maid of Athens". Her manuscript was her story. She wanted Jack to take it to England and find a publisher. With his habit of losing things he advised against it, but her powers of persuasion prevailed.

Meanwhile there was the sick girl to worry about. Having put her in the hands of a doctor, he decided the simplest thing would be to abandon her, even though it might cost him his big advance payment on the flat. Life in Rome was becoming too difficult, and in any case the films seemed now to be stalled. Bob and George had begun to pull his leg about *Hanger Lane* with talk of making Edna (Evelyn) black and re-titling the movie "I Sit on Brooklyn Bridge". Jack, however, took their suggestions seriously at the time; only years later did he realise they were probably having a little fun at his expense. But now important people had moved chairs at Warner Brothers-Seven Arts (the backers), one consequence of which was that Peter Sellers was lost. His reported week-long session spent perfecting Horace's (Jack's) Cambridgeshire accent would be wasted. No more script conferences were ever called after Rome and the two projects died of neglect, the most common fate of movie ideas, even good ones. And for Jack it meant there would be no sixty-four thousand dollar pay-off. In fact the first thing he did on his return to London was to borrow a hundred pounds from his son Peter.

Jack's publishers showed interest in the "Maid of Athens" story, but he didn't want the editing job and no alternative editor could be found. As predicted, he eventually lost the manuscript. Whenever he says that I instantly picture the missing item being accidentally dropped in the street or left on the train, but what he means is that it is lost somewhere in his current abode. Every few years, searching for something else in his plastic-bag Stacey Hill Farm archives, he will come across the Greek girl's account of her brief English fame. (He had to keep on telling her that he would send it back soon until she lost interest.) With about the same frequency he finds a long lost play, "The Long-Running Musical". This was to have been his big stage breakthrough, sometime in the sixties. The characters were all reviled fugitives from a popular soap opera who would risk being murdered if they ventured outdoors. The set was to be a gigantic grand piano, from the bowels of which the characters would emerge onto the stage. His producer telegrammed a confident message that they would open simultaneously on Broadway and in the West End. Then for some reason it suddenly died.

Maggie had sent Jack a birthday telegram in Rome. When he got home he was glad at last to have her there. She had won the contest with the Jersey girl - except of course that with only one active contender there hadn't really been a contest. So Jack and Maggie began to live together in a large front room of the big house on East Heath Road, Hampstead. In the near neighbourhood were many famous people in the arts: Peter O'Toole, Dudley Moore, Peter Cook, Marty Feldman, Alan Bates, Keith Michell, Peter Barkworth, to name a few, as they say. They would be encountered as very ordinary mortals in the pubs, shopping in Sainsbury's, on the streets in the rain (Jack remembers meeting Kingsley Amis, High-Noon fashion, in a wet, deserted street, each of them burdened with two carrier bags), stretching in a morning on the front doorstep as they brought in the milk, or wherever. Right next door to

Jack's house (actually fronting on Squire's Mount), was the home of Richard Burton's first wife Sybil, and several of the Jenkins brothers were near neighbours. Soon the house next door would be got ready to receive the most famous show-business couple in the world.

Jack Trevor Story, meanwhile, was moving into his own period of greatest fame. There were frequent television appearances on programmes like *Late Night Line-up*, more rave reviews of a quick succession of new novels, countless humorous pieces in *Punch,* a jazz column in the local *Ham and High*, and most important of all his Saturday column in the *Guardian*.

But Jack's novels of this period cannot be passed over; they should survive as his greatest achievement. He had gone to America with a second Horace novel, a sequel to *Hanger Lane*, part completed. Since returning, whether because of other commitments or a lack of inspiration, he was finding the book impossible to finish. But then came a fortuitous event that broke the blockage - fortuitous from a strictly literary point of view only. He and Maggie were picked up one winter's night by the police after he failed a breathalyser test. He became aggressive because they said she must stay in the car while he accompanied them to the station. On a dark night in Notting Hill it wasn't safe for a girl to be left alone in a car, especially if the doors couldn't be locked. (All of his cars, he says, have been like that; I don't know what happens to them but it's true of his current old Princess.) So after some arguing they were both taken along, Jack muttering insults all the way and refusing to give his name. What happened once they were inside the police station is graphically described - Maggie's account - in a contemporary newspaper report (*Kensington Post*). Evidently they were subjected to pretty rough treatment, Maggie especially, who reacted violently, so they said, and was later charged with assault and damage to property. There was a later, successful appeal against sentence, but the reality was that they were both badly shaken by the experience. He speaks of their nerves having been broken. He couldn't write for a while, but when he returned to it his writing personality had undergone a change. The unfinished Horace novel was transformed in consequence into an altogether wilder tale than *Hanger Lane*. Jack Trevor Story, with a little help from the police constabulary, had gone through yet another door.

One Last Mad Embrace cannot easily be summarised; one can only point to some of the people and happenings. Early on in the novel Horace is literally crucified - nailed to a tree on the Stevenage by-pass by mad film producer Norman Freville's henchmen in a dispute over a woman. He is dictating the book because the holes in his hands are still too painful to allow him to type. (After the book came out everyone wanted to see Jack's own - unmarked - palms.) With Horace through much of the action is Ariadne, a terrifyingly advanced nymphet - she has to remain at twelve so that her mother can stay twenty-nine - who bemuses him with her "purports" (fancied alternative lives). Then there is Albert Harris, his former milkman, who has infiltrated and risen to astonishing heights in the film business. Albert has supposedly been killed in a plane crash, but he makes a surprise appearance quite early in the plot. Much of the early action is in a Hampstead flat populated (as in the real case) almost entirely by females - nurses, actresses, stranger creatures - and always in the background are the domestic entanglements. Later there is a wild, extended car chase with Ariadne to the Hebrides. More pronounced in this novel than its predecessors is the helplessness of a central character who is seemingly at the centre of events, but can't control them, and notices how much better informed everyone else is than himself. This typical situation would recur in later books; one thinks of *Morag's Flying Fortress* (1976), and his unpublished novel *The Art of Dying*.

Seckers had published a further Jack Trevor Story title after *Hanger Lane* - the re-hashed Sexton Blake in which the famous detective becomes an MP, *Dishonourable Member*. They said they considered it one of his best books (without knowing its origins). Jack told them they had gone down as publishers in his estimation if they could think that. This exchange may have influenced their rejection now of *One Last Mad Embrace*, although they could simply have been scared of it. On Michael Moorcock's advice Jack approached Allison & Busby. They were evidently more adventurous, for the new book was immediately accepted. The reviews as ever were wonderful - and the sales ordinary. In the same year (1970) Allison & Busby published Jacks's third and last Horace Spurgeon Fenton novel, *Hitler Needs You*, in which the character's adolescent years (closely following Jack's own) are filled in. Invented are an unsolved murder and dark intimations of the impending holocaust. But the book draws well back from the kind of wild disorder so rampant in *One Last Mad Embrace*, demonstrating that in spite of his traumatic experience at Notting Hill police station, Story could still write when he put his mind to it in a relatively restrained manner more pleasing to the general reader. Indeed, the book was serialised in the *Cambridge Daily News* (whose features editor had a shock when he began to receive letters of complaint from real people whose names Jack hadn't bothered to change because he had assumed they had long since died).

Next though - in quick succession and dashed off in a temper while his driving ban was still in force - came two more extraordinary ventings of his paranoid fears and imaginings: *Little Dog's Day* and *The Wind in the Snottygobble Tree*, both published by Allison & Busby in 1971. The anger behind these books derived from the police ill-treatment; as to the paranoia, I am conscious that that part of his nature has rather disappeared from this narrative since I stopped dipping into Ross's manuscript. I have heard no tales of comparable behaviour in relation to his later women; most of the paranoia was evidently now going where it belonged - into his fiction. But the books were being fed also, I would say, by his recent experiences abroad; whether by chance or intention, he had

seemed always to be close to unseen but conceivably life-
threatening dangers.

Little Dog's Day and *The Wind in the Snottygobble Tree*
could both be classified as fantasy novels - except that Jack
Trevor Story's books have too many ordinary everyday little
human touches to belong wholly in that category. If there were
any such classification, they would properly belong under "pure
paranoia".

The first is a black novel of the future: Art Henry,
recovering from a bizarre transplant operation in which he has
been given a monkey's heart, wanders the streets playing his
lonely trumpet in search of his lost poodle. Everyone - former
employers, family - is keeping well back, expecting him to fall
down dead at any moment. They have in fact already begun to
divide his possessions, only to have him return inconveniently
from the brink. The world of the early chapters seems fairly
normal; only gradually does it become apparent that the
characters are living in a nightmarish police state in which the
people are divided into a privileged, increasingly test-tube bred
conforming class and an underclass of "freelings" in the
ghettos, who are subjected to chemical experiments from the air
(like crop spraying), and from time to time selectively
"Hitlerised", or cemented-over, when their activities threaten
the smooth running of the system. Compared with, say,
Nineteen Eighty-Four, or Alan Sillitoe's *Travels in Nihilon*, this
bleak future state is conveyed with marvellous economy; the
whole book only runs to little more than a hundred-and-fifty
pages. Auberon Waugh, writing in the *Spectator*, said of *Little
Dog's Day*:

> Pure delight from beginning to end . . . very much like
> Mr Orwell's *Nineteen Eighty-Four* but it is much better
> written, much funnier and enlivened by a most unusual
> imagination . . . I must award Mr Story a gold medal.

Even more compact, *The Wind in the Snottygobble Tree* has another new central character - Marchmont - a cowardly dreamer who, bored with his job in a travel agency, and (like the author) temporarily banned from driving, begins to make little demands on his tourist customers, such as to deliver a mysterious package to a Mr So-and-so, at present holidaying in a certain hotel in Dubrovnik. The contents of these packages are quite meaningless, but to his astonishment Marchmont soon begins to receive intimations that he has become an unwitting player in the lethal game of international espionage. Terrifying happenings follow in which the equally brutal police and security services are involved in a bizarre plot to replace the Pope - scheduled to visit Britain - with a deluded inmate from a lunatic asylum; the real Pope is to be electrocuted via his chamber pot when he relieves himself during his journeying in his "Popemobile". Somehow, after much appalling mayhem, a kind of normality is restored, though it is by no means a comfortable normality:

> In the marbled existence of the everyday tabloid world
> only the innocent are crucified. Marchy and Patsy would
> dance on, he with a new car, she with a new nose, to
> love and marriage and the happy endings of a package
> future; to the mewings and mouthings and biological
> stains and the pitter-patter of little club feet.

As to the "snottygobble tree" of the title, evidently that's a colloquial name for a species of yew ("Me?" cries Marchmont) in Jack Trevor Story's part of the world. Grown over refuse and given plenty of humous and an occasional dressing of dry blood, it produces slimy berries that you can't get off your hands if you squash them - poisonous, but said to be good for you if you don't eat them.

This novel, too, had ecstatic reviews; here is Robert Ray in *Books and Bookmen*:

The book possesses the kind of insanity which has the refreshing power of a bath of sulphuric acid, very badly needed in our neatly labelled, stereotype world.

And yet Allison & Busby would publish no further novels by Jack Trevor Story for nearly twenty years.

On 27 May 1972, only a few months before his world caved in with the discovery that Maggie, temping in Brussels, had fallen for another, Jack Trevor Story told his Saturday readers in the *Guardian* that the Burtons were moving back into the nondescript, bank-manager-size house next door - a house apparently built in the grounds of 18 East Heath Road, though fronting on the adjacent Squire's Mount. Their impending arrival was announced by the delivery, on the back of a lorry, of a ready-made garden. I used to think all the stuff about the Burtons next door, and the other celebrities living peaceful domestic lives in Hampstead, just like ordinary citizens, was made up, at least partly. Now I wonder what gave me that impression? Or who? The piece in question had the title "Diamond Liz and the Man from Next Door". Any other journalist would have made the famous couple the main topic of such an article. Story uses them merely as a way into a typically wide-ranging piece touching on a whole variety of other matters. The Burtons don't actually get much of a look in; which is not to say that the piece lacks interest. Here is Story on the development of movie technique:

> For me the movie was at its best in the days of the fixed camera when if the action went out of the frame you waited for it to come back . . . It seemed to me we were in a secret privileged hiding place, that the people on the screen didn't know we were there . . .

The sheer throw-away casualness of the references to the super-famous is what made them seem somehow improvised.

And Story knew what he was doing, for he had the odd person in his column sometimes question the veracity of these references, and then wait in vain for a straight answer. It was all art - but what the famous were said to have said or done had to be basically accurate. Even so, I have dipped into Melvyn Bragg's life of Richard Burton just to check that he and Liz Taylor did truly once live on Squire's Mount in Hampstead, and it's all there. (No mention of Burton's famous columnist neighbour, however.)

Jack always refers to his *Guardian column*, and it's a *single* column that I dimly remember. Yet a fair quantity of the pieces have recently come into my possession and I find that all these at any rate are spread over *several* columns. The *Guardian*, moreover, was a much thinner paper than it is today. Jack Trevor Story on this evidence had an extraordinary amount of space each Saturday to air his thoughts and generally ramble on in his inimitable way about his friends and family, his enthusiasms - and of course his Scottie girlfriend Maggie (though without conveying to his readers the depth now of his feelings for her). With today's demand for hard news and hard opinions, I don't suppose such freedom could be permitted now (his words were never cut or otherwise interfered with), even with all the extra space.

Everyone remembers Jack's very public agony over Maggie, but when you come to examine the pieces, like the Burtons she actually figures in his writing very little, making virtually no contribution to the topics he was airing each week. He has since been asked more than once to take Jack Trevor Story and Maggie on the stage, as if they were famous in print as a comedy double-act. But it wasn't so. I gather she was a pretty conventional girl who didn't much like having her name in the *Guardian* every Saturday (especially after they had parted company). Sometimes he even had to cover his typewriter when she was around for fear she might think he was writing about her again. She was unquestionably the love of his life; yet it seems a pity that his *Guardian* writing - in the opinion of many his best work - is remembered chiefly because of Maggie, sleeping behind that makeshift screen while Jack typed through the night.

Many of the best pieces were gathered in *Letters to an Intimate Stranger*, published by Allison & Busby in 1972, with Jack and Maggie on the cover in Edwardian dress, as they had appeared together for an item on Rupert Brooke in *Late Night Line-up*. The note at the front is very poignant:

> Written here in Hampstead overlooking the Vale, this book is the only child of our life together - me and Maggie and Poodle. It is dedicated to Michael McNay of the *Guardian* who, as principal midwife, encouraged its delivery chapter by chapter until the sad and dying fall of summer, 1972, when the room became empty.

And who can forget those sad, breakfast-time words of Jack's on his return from a nightmarish trip to Brussels to try to reclaim his girl?

> We are back in the continuing Story of painful place, folks, and I have to tell my regular readers that Maggie has fallen in love. I don't want to spoil your coffee or dampen your croissants with tears, but I have to break the sad news that Poodle is motherless.

Chapter Ten

DWARF GOES TO OXFORD

The grip that Jack could exert on his girls and womenfolk seems astonishing. Whether as a husband, father, or even lover, the evidence is that he performed poorly; and yet he could hold them in a kind of emotional force-field which they virtually had to go abroad to escape. Evelyn, for instance, in these years was still doing his washing (and hoping for him to come back to her). Ross (in her book) claims to have grown indifferent, though she isn't altogether convincing on that and there was still some contact. And Eunice, too, was still vaguely in touch. It was to her that Jack eventually turned in his despair after Maggie had made good her escape. She told him to come over to Jersey, where she would arrange accommodation for him with a friend, promised him pocket-money, and suggested he write a book about his grief to get Maggie out of his system. He took the dog with him; but Eunice seems actually to have wanted neither of them back. She was simply being a good friend in an hour of great need. His agony aside, Jack Trevor Story was a lucky man. And before he left he had another piece of good fortune: by chance he was approached on the street by a literate young girl from the north-east who had recognised him. The was Elaine Hepple - a true soul-mate at last (though it would take Jack some time to realise it), despite an age difference of around forty years. He told her he was off to Jersey for a spell to write a book, but suggested a dinner-date on his return. And such was his power of attraction, in combination with her pleasure at meeting him (she had once got into trouble at school for reading *The Wind in the Snottygobble Tree* in class), that the arrangement held.

In Jersey he wrote a novel as Eunice had recommended, *Crying Makes Your Nose Run*. The book wasn't a success in as much as both he and others felt that this was less than the definitive version of his heartbreak over Maggie. He claims to have dealt with it better in his next novel, *Morag's Flying Fortress*, though I wouldn't altogether agree. *Crying Makes Your Nose Run* was his dirtiest or most sexually explicit (depending how you like to think of it) book to date; it obeys, and even surpasses, Mr Emmanuel's old injunction that sexual intercourse should occur at least once every fourth page. Only ten years after the Lady Chatterley trial, it is amazing what authors could now get away with. And yet the book isn't in the least erotic. What is conveys most strongly is the raw emotion of *neurotic* love. The chief character is a jilted film producer, Ray "Cry Cry" Williams, who needs the support of an army of people to cope with his heartbroken condition. Services of every kind - psychiatric, sexual - are on offer, though to no avail. The man is inconsolable. Meanwhile the narrator, a scriptwriter much like Horace Spurgeon Fenton, though with the unlikely name of Edgar Wallace, is also enmeshed in a neurotic love affair. He is in a kind of agony of fear of loss even while his affair is flourishing. All this strikes me as being closer to Jack's likely emotional state in the aftermath of Maggie's departure from his life than the later book. (The title, incidently, he had actually got from Maggie herself some time earlier - so he once told me. One day on a journey she was in tears over something and said between sobs, "Crying makes your nose run!" Jack always has an ear for a good title, and a compulsion to make note of it before it's lost, as can so easily happen. While she sought to be comforted, he searched desperately for pencil and paper to jot it down. Such is the ascendancy in a writer's mind of art over life, at least while the going is good.)

Presumably because of unsatisfactory sales of the earlier books, Allison & Busby would not take *Crying Makes Your Nose Run* - which seems extraordinary, bearing in mind that Jack was writing regularly in the *Guardian* and *Punch* and was in short, for a writer, still (in his own phrase) "terribly famous". Was there something or someone else operating against him? Had he offended or outraged too many people in the business? Were there influential people at work who didn't like his public agonies over girls much younger than himself? I don't know, and it would be impossible to find out. But I would lean myself to the opinion that his writing was ahead of its time. A number of people have told me they used to find his *Guardian* stuff incomprehensible. I know I had difficulty with it myself at the time. Well, looking at the pieces now, I can't understand why anyone should have been baffled; though that may simply be a matter of familiarity. I don't know that I would want to argue that today's new generation of readers would find him less taxing. Jack Trevor Story's time may still lie in the future.

Crying Makes Your Nose Run might not have found a publisher at all had it not been for a chance conversation with a stranger in a pub with publishing connections. (Of course, such an encounter would not be so improbable in the Coach & Horses in Hampstead as it would be in a provincial pub.) At any rate the book was published in 1974 by David Bruce & Watson, with a neat dedication (Story should have written more poetry):

> How richly satisfying;
> A rival unprotected by the law of libel.
> For that truly lovely person, then,
> Temp's delight, Paul Waeben.
> Leaping, common market onion.
> Instant for anything that rustles.
> A clerk, or some such, with BICAL. Brussels.

Such reviews as I have seen are favourable enough, but the book wasn't a best-seller, needless to say.

I may as well confess at this point something which will in fact already be apparent to the reader, namely, that I have not been

successful in contacting and extracting the opinions of any of
the three principal women in Jack Trevor Story's life after his
family relationships. The lady in Jersey I wrote to at an
address given me by Jack, and I know she received that letter
because she has since talked to him on the phone and mentioned
it. Later I wrote again and this time my letter was returned by
the GPO, undelivered. I could have tried phoning at some
point myself, of course, but instead I let it go. Even though the
lady in question has kept up a distant friendship with Jack, she
is the one I would say who was most damaged by her
association with him, and therefore the one deserving most
consideration. However she feels about him these days, it is
plain enough that she has no wish to talk at all, never mind with
any eagerness. And after all, what could she say? The worst
would be that the man was an absolute swine - with chapter and
verse. But that is hardly new information. One of the odd
things about Jack Trevor Story is that despite being a vain man
he is quite ready to tell or concede the worst about himself.
Later in the seventies, for instance, when he was writing for
Radio Times, Ross was incensed by something in an article and
wrote to the editor explaining just what kind of man he really
was. The editor approached him nervously to ask if he would
mind if the letter were printed. To his surprise, Jack readily
conceded that he had been a complete shit with Ross (his word
talking to me) and offered no resistance at all. On the contrary,
he said he *loved* that kind of thing. Such an attitude effectively
neutralises anything his ex-girlfriends might conceivably want
to throw at him. So, what would be the point of causing
embarrassment - and conceivably pain - to any of these women
in their new lives? I wrote to Maggie at an old address in
Scotland and got neither a reply nor the letter returned. I think
that's enough, all these years later. (He hasn't seen or heard
from her since the 1972 confrontation in the Brussels flat,
although she did return once to Hampstead when he was absent
to try to recover clothes she had left there. In a brief fit of the
old paranoia, he had locked them in the boot of his car against

this possibility; but later he relented and forwarded everything to Brussels via a friend.) Elaine I don't have an address for, nor a married name if she has married again. She has been gone for seven or eight years now, without any contact with Jack. I can't believe she would be any more eager to cooperate than the others if she *were* contactable, even though by all accounts she is - or was - a very different kind of woman. Jack persists in believing that these ex-girlfriends are somehow an organic part of his life still ("Elaine would throw up if she heard you say that," he said to me recently, over some clumsy remark). My own unsophisticated and doubtless provincial view is that having spent with him a fair part of their youth, they are entitled now to be left in the privacy they obviously prefer. I don't mean to suggest that they were wasted years; on the contrary, it is very likely that Jack Trevor Story was and will remain the most vital thing that ever happened to them. But time moves on. The Jersey lady I have given a false name for protection. Maggie and Elaine have been written about far too much already for there to be any point in falsifying theirs.

So, that said, we are now into the seventies. Still convalescing somewhat from his nervous breakdown over Maggie, Jack Trevor Story is soon joined in the Hampstead flat on his return from Jersey by this very young but life-experienced girl from the north-east. She is taken on the visiting round of friends, relatives and old haunts - introduced as his new girlfriend, even though everyone must understand that his love for Maggie is undiminished. The much-travelled dog, having had to adapt to a change of name (Beauty to Poodle), must now accustom itself to a new, third, mother. Jack is continuing to write for television, moving on from such as *No Hiding Place* to better quality drama like *Public Eye* and *Budgie*, besides contributing the occasional original play (one is a strong contender for the British entry for Montreux but has to be withdrawn because its police murder theme is too close to a story in the headlines). The work, however, is beginning to dry up. In the book field his itch to put off the general reader, and at the same time in effect to begin his career over again with each new and different novel, is putting off the publishers, too, with the result that he is finding it next to impossible to place his new work. But his stuff is still being printed in the newspapers and magazines - the *Guardian* will last until beyond the mid-seventies and *Punch* (the best thing that ever happened to him, he now says; in particular because of its willingness to publish so many of his more serious short stories in addition to all the humorous pieces) through to the late-eighties as reliable outlets for his work. On television as a performer, too, he remains in demand, usually under the direction of the husband-and-wife team John and Pat Ingram; later in the decade this will lead to his own prime-time series. Evelyn and Ross, meanwhile, are living out their lives in some solitude now that all the children are grown up. Evelyn continues to live in the old council house on Meadway in Welwyn Garden City; Ross has sold the big house on Arundel Drive in Worthing and settled in Eastbourne. Neither, sadly, has very long to live.

Jack was discharged from bankruptcy at some point in the early seventies - as part of a general amnesty for some of the older and more stubborn cases, as he explains it. But then, in 1974, came a second receiving order. Claims, mainly to the Inland Revenue, this time totalled in excess of twenty-four thousand pounds - a figure later reduced, as if by magic (or creative accounting), to less than five. But the publicity was proving useful. After years of straining to achieve fame as a writer, he finally made it instead as a bankrupt. Sales of his books increased a little, and there was someone else to worry about the money and the numbers. About the only inconvenient thing was that he had to drop plans to be a director of a proposed local radio company. The bankruptcy experience was a handy source of raw material, too. Others facing it earnestly sought his advice, and given the general fascination with the subject he could sometimes respond in the form of a newspaper article. In one *Guardian* piece - "Hallelujah I'm a Bum" - he answered a reader's entire detailed questionnaire, though it is doubtful if his advice gave his conventionally minded correspondent the kind of reassurance he was hoping for:

If you're really going to join us it doesn't matter whether you catch up on your tax and National Insurance payments or not - you put one lot of people in touch with another lot of people and they give each other something to do; it doesn't really concern you.

But despite this carefree attitude, money had still to be earned. "You can never replace a salary," he often says. "The moment I gave up my Marconi wage I was in trouble, and it's been that way ever since." Story's job on *Radio Times* - for several years in the mid-seventies - seems to have been as a kind of staff writer, which was by no means beneath him. In fact he was one of a number of writers with names recruited by the magazine. They went out on assignments to talk to and be photographed with people involved in the making of new or topical programmes and to write a kind of preview. But he was able to use a personal angle - to work his own attitudes, passions and humour into the pieces. This was really the first proper journalism he had ever done - hack work of a sort, though it was a pleasure to get away from the indoor desk and typewriter and to travel the country at someone else's expense. Often young Elaine went along with him. The assignments included a stint on the beat - or rather in the panda-cars - of the coppers policing Castleton, high up in the Peak District (no sign of his paranoid feelings about the police in the resulting piece); an interview with actress Rachel Roberts, immersed in a play about a self-sufficient old woman living a hermit-like life on a hillside in Wales (this pre-dated the emergence of Yorkshire's Hannah Hauxwell as a television celebrity); a visit to Holmfirth to meet the *Last of the Summer Wine* gang; and most poignantly, an encounter with the friends and fellow mental-hospital inmates who had assisted Joey Deacon, a fifty-four year old spastic, in the great labour of writing a book about his life spent entirely in institutions - at a moment when the value of such places was at last beginning seriously to be questioned. With a handicapped daughter in his own life, this was an assignment that Jack could approach with some passion:

> You lot with your jobs and wages and no sugar probably
> know nothing of the great nationwide circuit of the afflicted.
> Cripples, spastics, big-headed, crooked-spined, deaf, dumb,
> the idiot, simple or borderline intelligent whom most of us
> prefer not to mention. They live out their lives, out of sight,
> out of mind, in places like St Lawrence's.

Well, they don't any longer, not so many of them anyway, here in 1991. He ought to report that.

(Notice that "no sugar", incidently; for me it's the writer of genius showing through. Story is saying in those two words, I believe, that the rest of us are too busy tending to the needs of our already healthy bodies to spare these suffering people a moment of our precious thoughts.)

But this *Radio Times* work wasn't a full-time occupation; he was still freelancing and writing novels (even without a prospective publisher). Commissions aside, he has in general preferred to write for himself rather than to please an editor or publisher, although he will sometimes pick up a topical subject that interests him for an article. The consequence is that a great deal of Story's later output in particular remains unpublished - abandoned when he ran out of money for postage and return of the manuscript. With bulky novels, this has always been a very practical consideration. Surprisingly, for an established author who has published so much, he has tended to lack the courage to pick up the phone and chat to an editor in advance of submitting a manuscript. Writers of his acquaintance whose names are not so well known as his have been far more successful in commercial terms, and in the avoidance of wasted effort, by virtue of an assiduously professional approach to marketing their writing. Only very recently (as I write) has he begun seriously to use the phone to sell his work; currently his daughter Jacqueline, whose job has given her the right kind of persuasive telephone manner, is acting as intermediary (a better agent than most he has known).

Back in the seventies, though, with his novels in particular, Story had the arrogance still (the other side of his cowardice) to believe that his name alone on a manuscript would be what counted when it arrived on an editor's desk. In reality, for partly mysterious reasons, it was beginning to be the thing that put the editor off. His next novel, *Morag's Flying Fortress* (1976), almost failed to reach print; only an unaccountable alignment of favourable circumstances finally persuaded Hutchinson to publish the book - without, as I understand it, a paperback tie-in, which was becoming essential to protect the hardback publisher's investment. The novel nevertheless, besides much else, has what are surely Jack Trevor Story's best ever opening sentences:

> It was on of those mornings when everything rhymes.
> It's not that all the troubles and confusions and un-
> certainties are not still there. What you've got to do
> is wake up with amnesia. Your mind is untangled.
> The paths that kept going sideways now lie right
> ahead,   the late autumn flowers blend with simple
> colours, a breeze presses comfortably chill on the skin
> of your face and neck, your hair stirs tangibly on your
> scalp. Between the high villas and the high trees the
> sun hangs in a smoke-blue void without shining, as
> comfortable to look at with your clear eye as a frosted
> hundred-watt lamp. Order has come out of chaos, you
> are again a part of the universe and alive. Very likely
> there will be more con-fusions by lunchtime but you
> will not get caught up in them because you are in
> control again. Yesterday's mad-ness has gone.

Curiously (or not so curiously bearing in mind Story's own industrial past) these lines are written by an electronics engineer and technical author narrator, Alec Ranger, who is emerging from the pain of a nervous breakdown over a girl - or is it something deeper and more mysterious? The writing soon settles into a more workmanlike kind of prose, so that the reader begins to believe he is reading quite a straightforward tale about editors of and contributors to technical journals. But of course unsettling things soon begin to happen to Alec - why is everyone worried about what he is doing for Christmas? Why do his friends appear to watch him and keep popping up in unexpected places? In the mental background is a supposedly historical event - the crashing during the war of a Flying Fortress bomber; not in Belgium, as thought, but only twelve miles from Ipswich town hall. Is this bomber in Alec Ranger's head, or in the mind of technical editor Geoffrey Neasden's mystically insane daughter Morag? Well, Alec it appears is a seeded spy who doesn't know he's been seeded - which is about as far as I can go with this brief analysis of a highly complex novel. I have seen printouts of Story's library lending figures, and *Morag's Flying Fortress* has been one of his most borrowed books. Forgive me if I sound surprised, but I do wonder what all those thousands of readers made of the book. For the fact is that I know something none of them could have known, namely that the drug thalidomide figured importantly in *Morag's Flying Fortress* as first written - a secret Nazi weapon. This was too controversial and the references had to be removed - quite late - leaving a somewhat baffling if beautifully written tale of what looks like mainly madness. (Story has been told that his later novels don't work because *everyone* is insane; there is no fixed point of sanity. I would comment that the leading character is always in a different *camp* from the people around him, and mad at least in a different way from them, if mad at all.)

In 1977 came the move for Jack and Elaine to Stacey Hill Farm upon his appointment as writer in residence for Milton Keynes. Poodle went, too, although she died of old age (and possibly an excess of readjustment) soon afterwards. The move attracted a good deal of publicity in the media - or Jack was able to exploit it for that purpose. At any rate interviews or articles appeared in many newspapers, including the *Sunday Times* and the *Observer*, and of course the *Guardian*. There were several television films and shorter pieces too: *One Man's Week* and *Personal Report*, to mention two. Milton Keynes' new town sprawl, with its endless system of tightly integrated roads and roundabouts, was then in mid-development, with many of the roads still mud, cut into irreplaceable green fields. The concept was a difficult one to feel enthusiastic about at that particular moment. Jack took the camera around the wasteland, talking negatively - and biting the new hand that was feeding him. It was too late for those who had appointed him to do much about this, but since the appointment was for only a year, they thought it was only a matter of waiting until he was at last free to leave the ghastly town upon termination of his contract; then they would be able to put the spacious upper-floor flat of the old farmhouse at the disposal of those organising the collection of industrial and rural life. But at the end of the year to everyone's surprise Jack had a change of heart or mind - or maybe he checked his wallet (as a bankrupt still he wasn't permitted a bank account). He now said publicly that he had developed a taste for living in the country and wanted to stay on at Stacey Hill Farm. He and Elaine had begun to cultivate the garden at the back of the house and had already put in vegetables. They were in short putting down roots. It is hard to believe that the Development Corporation can have tried hard to evict them; maybe because Jack had after all been so successful at bringing publicity to this huge and costly enterprise way out in the middle of nowhere. Fourteen years later he is still living there.

As a result of the success of *Personal Report* and *One Man's Week*, Jack was invited in 1978 to do an extended series of personal programmes, six in all, for ATV. They were to be based, however, on his *Guardian* writings rather than the despoliation of the Buckinghamshire countryside. The result was *Jack on the Box*, to be screened at 9pm each Thursday evening in the summer of 1979. Each episode had a title: *Death - Work - Love & Marriage - Money - Patriotism - Fear*, but these headings were only a loose guide; the topics had a tendency to dissolve into a surreal autobiography of the author. His lost love Maggie was a running theme through the series; usually she appeared as an apparition, as when Jack was gazing down into the water below a bridge in Burwell. For the third episode he gathered together his children, and with the lead that he had been writing about them for long enough invited them to unburden themselves as frankly as they wished. The result was mixed. In general the older children (Evelyn's) were more forgiving, while the younger ones were bitter. He also found time in the programmes to talk one-to-one with an assortment of guests such as Sir Freddie Laker, the Dean of Westminster, Barbara Cartland, and his old pal Bill Johnson.

In the midst of all this filming, Evelyn was taken into hospital, mortally ill as it transpired. Some months before she had had a long operation to repair a perforated eardrum, from which she had emerged partially paralysed. In this condition she had managed to live on alone without too much difficulty, even though she was also by now suffering from heart trouble. For this latter condition she was evidently inclined to experiment with her drug intake, and this may have been a contributory cause of her sudden illness during the filming. The crisis came as the younger family were gathered for the *Love and Marriage* episode, immediately after which Lee also went down with a mysterious illness and was rushed into intensive care. Only a day or two after all this drama Jack had to travel to France with actress Michelle Newell (playing

Maggie) and the camera crew to renew the search for his father's grave and pretend to care.

Jack on the Box attracted much favourable comment (usually with photographs) in all the papers, but after its interruption by the technicians' strike of that summer ATV proved unwilling to run the full series again. Instead the three unscreened programmes were shown late at night some considerable time afterwards, making nonsense of the continuity. Viewers are forever complaining about repeats, but in the years since *Jack on the Box* has never been repeated; nor, to the puzzlement of a great many people, has Story been invited to do a follow-up series of any kind. It's another mystery - as is the fact that only the tiny Manchester-based publishers Savoy Books came forward to do a tie-in book (a paperback); this for a fully networked prime-time six-episode television show. Someone up there evidently doesn't like Jack Trevor Story.

Meanwhile the rejected novels were beginning to pile up. To follow *Morag's Flying Fortress*, Jack next offered Hutchinson *The Art of Dying* - a surreal tale of the misadventures of a struck-off doctor. His memory (which can be faulty) is that the manuscript, later rejected, was at first received with enthusiasm. The novel remains unpublished to this day, except for extracts which have appeared in *World Medicine*.

Also doing the rounds was *Up River*. After countless rejections, with the help of an intermediary the book was accepted by Colin Haycraft at Duckworth and published in 1979. A long-standing complaint about Jack Trevor Story's writing is that he too often goes over the top. In *Up River* he pushed this tendency to the limit - the book's first title was "The Screwrape Lettuce". Unusually for him the leading character is a woman, Caroline Latimer. She is an unattractive nymphomaniac who complains that she has been attacked many times, but never for her body. Based loosely on an upper crust lady of Jack's acquaintance, Caroline has surely the foulest female tongue in all of literature. Here she is talking to her interfering mother on the phone:

> "Fuck off you nosey cow. Where did you get this fucking number? I told you never to ring me at my friends' houses. You piss up my life. You pissed up Warren. You pissed up David. Every man I have you piss it up. All that middle-class fucking greed. Cross-examining them about their prospects. Fuck off, mummy."

But poor frustrated Caroline is about to come into her own, for off-stage strange things are happening. A plague of permanent erections is blowing in from the Urals, emanating from a mysterious strain of red lettuce developed by the Russians to enhance rabbit breeding. Infected first is a special police force, and soon Caroline encounters the cuddly but insatiably rampant Ben Dobbin, who talks in joined-up words ("Gorjamarvellous!")

Well, if you read *Up River* without ever understanding that it is a book about police brutality, you haven't read it all, says Jack. The permanent erections and the free use these rampaging constables are able to put them to represent our boys in blue and their tendency to wade into crowds of defenceless people, truncheons flailing.

Can one accept this? Once again the novel isn't in the least erotic. Always, Jack explains, there is a strong medical element in the sexual happenings he writes about which neutralises their pornographic content. And of course in *Up River* it isn't long before the reader begins to feel decidedly sorry for Dobbin and his sorely afflicted pals. Later, remedies more desperate than mere rape are resorted to, not excluding crude amputation. In writing the novel Story surely wasn't intending to arouse or titillate his readers, therefore; but even so, many people would consider it an outrageously dirty book. Reviews in my possession suggest that the critics were divided on this point. The *Guardian* rather dismissed it as the product of a filthy mind, while in the *Sunday Times* Peter Ackroyd described *Up River* as "volatile, grotesque, brilliantly messy - like watching a diamond burst in the hand".

The late 1979-1980 period was a time of terrible illness in Jack Trevor Story's family life. Lee's sickness was some rare kind of pneumonia, which for a time looked as if it might be fatal. Frantic with anxiety after a hospital visit one night, Ross (his mother) killed a horse on a dark country road in her Morris Minor Traveller. For a strong animal lover who was also a cowboy writer, this was a profoundly - spiritually - upsetting experience. Shortly afterwards (Lee having thankfully recovered) it was discovered that she had cancer, though whether this could be attributed to the accident is impossible to say. At any rate it was the beginning of a surprisingly brief period of operations, unpleasant treatments, false hopes and hopeless misery, leading finally to her death in the spring of 1980. One gathers that Ross was a difficult woman, kinder perhaps to animals than to people. Jack calls her a martinet. She had house rules of behaviour - no smoking, no watching anything rude on television - which she applied with unthinking ruthlessness. During her last illness she was moved around the family, never really settling anywhere. She even spent time with Jack and Elaine at Stacey Hill Farm. At the end she went voluntarily into a hospice, where there was a better guarantee of a peaceful atmosphere. In the years separated from Jack, having sold the Worthing house she had lived in Eastbourne, then spent several years in London working with Bill Howard Baker. More recently she had settled at Sandhurst, close to Lee's home at Bodiam Castle. To the end she was still writing - in her head after writing on paper became impossible. Jack remembers her waking from a coma, worried chiefly about what was to happen to "Jake", a character in her new book. After her death titles under various pen-names (Catherine Tracy, Richard Jeskins, Charles H Wood, Desmond Reid) continued to appear, though a publisher could not be found for her autobiography. She is buried in a high graveyard near Bodiam, known to the family as "Boot Hill".

Meanwhile Jack's own health was showing signs of deterioration; but just before that too became a serious matter there was a brighter moment when he was freed from bankruptcy. Although being bankrupt had its advantages, most beneficial from the publicity point of view was to pass into or out of the bankrupt state. After five years there was little mileage left in continuing to be bankrupt; but the papers were predictably eager to report his discharge. According to the *Times* report he almost missed his appointment with the official receiver after lingering too long over lunch with Robert and Sheridan Morley, but that seems to have caused him little anxiety. The discharge agreement was that he would pay ten-per-cent of his future earnings to his creditors for a period of three years, which seems fairly painless. Much as this appears to have been quite a happy moment, there is no sign that Jack was planning to mend his ways.

"I can get into debt again now - the cost of living has gone up since I last had a cheque book in 1967," he told the reporters on leaving court. "I am going to find myself one of those marvellous credit cards, get myself a loan, and buy a Range Rover on HP". And more philosophically, he added:

"Getting discharged from bankruptcy is like getting your wings back. It is getting your soul back. I used to have a big soul, a soul as big as my Jaguars and Armstrong Siddeleys and six-litre Galaxie convertible automatic. Now my soul does 50mpg after all these nervous, careful, law-abiding years. It is a horrible little Renault 6 soul."

But it was a little Renault 6 with a big heart that carried Jack around during his own time of awful illness in the spring and summer months of 1980, when quite frequently his legs were close to useless.

His sudden ill health brought Jack into sharp conflict with the medical profession, much of which is recorded in a long and bitter article published in *World Medicine* in October 1980, called "A Fight for Survival in the NHS Jungle", which many readers took for humour.

Till then all he had really known was his usual nervous asthma. To be helpful, he mentioned this long-standing complaint to his doctors (it never seemed to be the same one) and from there asthma became what was wrong with him, even though the real problem was incipient heart failure coupled with a lung infection - possibly heading for pleurisy or pneumonia, though again that was only Jack trying to help by revealing his tendencies. With the recent media publicity on what an awful place Milton Keynes was, he wasn't in any case in the good books of the local services, social or medical; though whether that contributed to the failure of his doctors to treat him properly, or if his paranoia was simply coming through too strongly, one cannot tell. But even Elaine was finding it hard to get a proper hearing. The official verdict, supported by X-rays, was that his lungs were perfect and his heart merely slightly enlarged (normal for an older man). There was also in the system the information that he had recently seen a cardiologist and been pronounced fit and well. This, however, was an administrative error: on the day in question he and Elaine had in fact been with Ross at the hospice, turning her over and over to relieve the pain of her cancer. But the missed appointment had been interpreted as a problem - if any - gone away. Meanwhile Jack's body was filling with water. His legs were swollen close to elephantiasis dimensions, and to get some air into his waterlogged lungs at night he was hanging with his elbows from the headboard of the bed in the crucifixion position.

Then Bill Johnson and his girlfriend and mother decided it would be a good idea to have a holiday, with Jack and Elaine included, choosing a cottage way down in Ilfracombe. Somehow he managed to drive there, but he was so ill that a local doctor was consulted. This new man at last made a correct diagnosis and gave him the drugs he needed to get rid of the water and regularise the heartbeat. Jack quotes this doctor (the only one to come out of the article well) as saying, wisely, "The ills of the human body are too subtle, complicated and vernacular to be treated like something wrong with a lawnmower." (God help us when we are finally handed over entirely to computers for diagnosis!)

But that was by no means the end of the matter. When well enough, he was moved from the holiday cottage to Lee's home at Bodiam Castle. From there, on precisely the depressing day of Peter Seller's death, he drove to see a heart specialist in Tunbridge Wells, who told him for the first time, and with emphasis, that he had suffered serious heart failure. This put him into sustained shock. Believing he was dying for sure, and with care of his archives paramount in his mind, he suggested to Elaine that they get married. Ross had really been the one who had prevented him from marrying any of his girls, though chiefly on Evelyn's account. She had always felt guilty about taking him away from Evelyn, and had remained conscious of how important her marriage to Jack (which had never been dissolved) still was to her. Jack had hoped to marry again, if he ever did, in better circumstances; but with his legs barely under control he drove with Elaine down to Hastings, which was the nearest place where the job could be done. They tried to buy a ring first, but hadn't sufficient money for even the cheapest. Afterwards they returned to Bodiam, and while a celebration of sorts began Jack was put to bed, too ill to participate, although he looks surprisingly well in the photographs.

From Lee's cottage they transferred to what Jack describes as a little "folly-bungalow" in Peter's garden at Berkhamsted. He was still in a state of shock, so that the slightest disturbance brought on a fearful reaction. A little later, as part of a plan to return to Stacey Hill Farm by stages, he was driven up to see a cardiologist in Stony Stratford. In the middle of the recording he literally died. The pen on the chart ceased to move, while Jack found that he could not talk or move his limbs. Elaine chased around for a doctor and emergency heart massage was applied, the pulse soon happily being restored.

"Has this happened before?" the doctor asked when the drama had subsided.

"It happens every morning when I take my pills," said Jack.

It emerged that he had been overdosing on a drug designed to *slow* the heartbeat, but not to stop it altogether.

Since that time he has been kept alive and reasonably healthy by drugs. Nowadays, though, the cocktail is a simpler mix than it was for a time in that giddily terrifying summer of 1980.

Amongst the planned summer activities for 1980 which illness prevented were (according to Jack's *World Medicine* piece) sailing, hang-gliding and six months' work in San Francisco. He was also suffering from his recurrent hernia problem, which makes the more physical of these plans seem improbable - though that makes no allowance for his capacity, by skilled improvisation, to extend the range of things a man in a truss could manage. I don't know in fact if he ever got to sail or hang-glide, but I do know that after a longish period of recuperation he made a visit to California at some point in the early eighties.

By a roundabout route, this trip was linked to the success of the film *Ghandi*. The script had been written by Jack Briley, who had won an Oscar for it. Briley was an old chum of Story's; they had collaborated long ago on the Spike Milligan films. Now with the acclaim *Ghandi* had received, he was a hot property. In prospect was a film at last of Story's novel *Man Pinches Bottom*, written in the fifties. Options on this book had been sold before - once with Richard Attenborough in line for the part of Percey Paynter, the picture-comic artist whose dismissal for pinching a wrong bottom in a lift leads, after a hysterical newspaper campaign in which he is misrepresented as a child molester, to his near-murder by a gang of demented housewives. Producer Duane Hartzell was now interested and early work on the project was advanced by telephone. Eventually, with the chance of a Jack Briley script and Dudley Moore now in the Percey Paynter role, Jack flew out to Hollywood with his son Lee. He had had some past contact with Dudley Moore (and Peter Cook) in Hampstead; they had collaborated on a play based on his novel *Hitler Needs You*, which none of them had been able to set up. Dudley Moore had been very big in Britain back then; now, with the success of his film *Arthur*, he was tremendously big in Hollywood. Too big and too much in demand in fact to give much more than a moment's attention to this *Man Pinches Bottom* proposal. After this setback, father and son concentrated on having a good time out in California, which was only marginally inconvenienced by Jack's need to wear a complicated giant pad of a truss incorporating rolled-up hats to keep his guts in place for the more athletic pursuits. Most memorable and enjoyable were San Francisco, Berkeley, Tina Turner in concert, watching the filming of a *Dukes of Hazard* sequence in a little make-believe town with a main street blackened from squealing tyres, lunches with Jack Briley and his brother Bud, ferrying around the Golden Gate, and seeing a girl drown in the bay - which only Jack noticed. It was his hernia that finally brought them home, or rather an unexpected summons for a long-awaited operation. To keep the film alive in any case, it was looking as though Jack would have to write the script himself, and this he was unwilling to do. I understand that he may have turned his back on fifty-thousand dollars, though I suppose that could easily have turned out to be the usual big-money mirage.

Back home, no longer able to find an established publisher for his work, Story had begun to think of publishing his books himself. The new release of Hitchcock's film of *The Trouble with Harry* at the Queen Elizabeth Hall in November 1983 was a spur to setting up this enterprise. The book was out of print and it looked like an opportunity to cash in on the publicity.

Leveret Press was financed by two-thousand pounds from the BBC for some *Doctor Who* scripts, six hundred for a *Budgie* repeat, and an injection of five thousand from his son Peter, who had a prosperous photography studio in Soho. Elaine was with him at the outset, but by the time *The Trouble with Harry* in its new edition was published in 1985 they had split, she having wandered off by degrees into university life. The book is beautifully put together, direct from the Macmillan (American) format and illustrations, but spoiled by a spoof foreword by "F Booker-Price". I say spoiled, but Jack wouldn't see it that way. Even with such a large sum of money at stake he was eager to thumb his nose at the literary establishment. Maybe for that reason, the book wasn't much remarked upon by reviewers. It proved very hard to market, the famous title notwithstanding. At precisely that same moment I was trying to stimulate interest in my William Saroyan anthology, *The New Saroyan Reader*, an American publication sold in Britain through an obscure distributor. I had obtained a list of public library addresses throughout the British Isles and was patiently writing letters to the most important ones. Jack asked for a copy of the list and began to follow suit, reaching out as far as little towns in the west of Ireland. But neither of us as I remember had much success in terms of sales, which was especially mystifying in the case of his offering. I think, though, that by one means or another he did finally dispose of most of his print run; at any rate I haven't seen them around at Stacey Hill Farm on my visits.

Jack had planned to reprint *I Sit in Hanger Lane*, but perhaps sensing that the writing was on the wall for Leveret he moved ahead quickly instead with a new title. He had a number of rejected novels to choose from, which he had hoped to print one by one under the Leveret imprint, alternating with successful reprints of his more famous old titles. But he decided to set the novels aside in favour of a just-completed memoir of the break-up of his marriage to Elaine Hepple. *Dwarf Goes to Oxford* deals so comprehensively with their relationship that I don't want to go over the same ground, even in outline. The parts of the book I like, Jack himself will probably be least proud of. Even so, here is something from the next-to-last page, on Elaine's grandparents in the north-east:

> They died, Florence and James, over these same years as
> our marriage dying. Blanchlands is a place of the past, in
> the snow and in the hot summers, Grandma Hepple, almost
> upside down with arthritis but busy as a beetle taking care
> of her Edwardian oasis and fettling visiting Arabs, no matter
> how many, with plentiful teas and pass the cakes and try
> the jam, the jelly, see the holy quiet in Dwarf's small eyes,
> weighing the fruit and measuring the sugar and never saying
> fuck - because Blanchlands is where she all began, as a little
> girl, when mummy was away.

The thousand or so books that remain are piled in neat rows in Jack's upper-storey flat, threatening to break the floor. But he is glad still to have them now. They have become Elaine herself - his Golden Girl.

Through the late eighties Jack Trevor Story and I wrote to each other a great deal. We did it without any real meeting of minds, neither really knowing who or what the other was and making surprisingly little attempt to find out. My own letters I imagine were dull, but even so they always brought a quick response - by which I mean a letter always came quickly back, often several pages of uncorrected single-space typing, with hand-scrawled extra messages in the margins. And since I couldn't leave a personal letter unanswered, I would write back again. Jack's letters were full of what was happening in his apparently busy life, and although they were frequently very funny, often I couldn't be sure who all the people were and what their connection was with him. Still, they were infinitely more stimulating than the rest of the stuff that drops through your letterbox day after day, so even after I had begun to suspect that his personal letters were perhaps early morning exercises for his mind and typing fingers I didn't discourage them. On the contrary, I felt privileged to be on the receiving end of his stream-of-consciousness ramblings. I suppose I even wondered from time to time if the letters might be valuable one day.

I had first written to Jack back in 1978, when he was in the middle of filming *Jack on the Box*. Until I actually met him in 1987, I hadn't really focused on what it might mean to be a writer in modern Britain who had slipped quite a way now from a position of considerable fame and was finding it very hard to make a living. Stacey Hill Farm itself was unexpectedly impressive, I discovered. Jack I found hard at work on an article for *Punch*. He had a few coins lying on the table beside his typewriter which at that moment he confessed were all the money he had in the world. And not only did he appear to be close to penniless; he seemed isolated, too, with no new girlfriend yet in sight to replace Elaine. Maybe I had called at the wrong time, but on subsequent visits I noticed that Stacey Hill Farm was always pretty deserted. Horribly naive and insulting as it now seems, a vague part of my motive in embarking on this biography was to do something to bring Jack Trevor Story in from the cold.

Chapter Eleven

A YEAR IN THE LIFE

That was the expectation - to spend about a year on the book.
It has overrun by eight months, but that hardly matters because
I am not writing to a deadline. In point of fact, since Jack
Trevor Story was incommunicado from roughly August 1990
through to the following March, making progress impossible,
with only a short way to go now I could fairly claim to be close
to finishing the book on schedule. The reader will have
probably gathered that Jack has survived and is still (November
1991) in residence at Stacey Hill Farm. Last winter it looked to
be in the balance.

The project began easily enough. Jack himself was always
going to be my chief source of information, since no one else in
the whole world knew his life in anything like the kind of detail
I needed. I suspect at the outset he had hopes that this wouldn't
be necessary; that from his letters, books, journalism, and
talking to people in his life I would be able to put together his
life story with minimal assistance from him. Well, I have made
as much use as possible of all the written material I could lay
my hands on, but with that alone I would soon have been
struggling. I managed interviews with such members of his
family as I could reach; others I wrote to ignored my letters.
Few people of course enjoy letter writing these days, but when
I turned to show-business and media folk I found them for the
most part uncooperative, too, even professional writers. Had I
had to rely on them I would have got nowhere. With Jack
himself still accessible, at least in the early stages, it seemed
increasingly pointless to try to prise odd little snippets of near-
useless information out of people who were preoccupied with
their own affairs. The book, I decided, would have to be more
of a collaborative effort than I myself had envisaged. How else

was I to get the basic framework of the events of his life, which was the very minimum requirement? And since Jack himself would certainly never write a straight *auto*biography, what after all was wrong with collaboration? The reason why in most biographies you read so much of what other people have to say is because the subject is usually dead, or unwilling to cooperate.

At the start I had some anxiety that Jack might be a difficult interviewee. My approach, if I was ever to have a chance of making sense of what he had to tell me, would have to be simply to work through all the different stages of his life in an orderly way. In his autobiographical writings he pays little attention to chronology, so there was quite a danger that he would be unwilling or unable to stay with the particular period I wished to explore. But I needn't have worried; he fell into it without the slightest protest or trouble, digressing only on rare occasions and then to tell me something out of context that I was glad to know anyway.

I soon found, though, that in spite of the nature of these sessions, Jack had little idea of the kind of book I was beginning to write. Even after I had sent him a few chapters he seemed to think I ought to be able to bung in extraneous stuff as it came along, without regard to where I happened to be in the narrative, and to make sudden changes of direction or tone if I wasn't happy with the way the book was going - anything in fact to break it up and stop the reader having an easy time. I told him loudly and firmly - but vainly - that I had no choice but to proceed doggedly with the course I had set if I was to have a hope of reaching the end. Mastering the material and getting it down in entertaining and readable form was task enough, given the fearful complexity of his life. To shake it all up and rearrange it in a kind of chronological mosaic even as I tried to assimilate it was beyond my powers. He thought I ought to be able to write with real feeling, too, about people who were very remote from the circumstances of my own life, complaining that I was simply moving cardboard characters around on a chess board. I argued that you could put such feelings into fiction, but not into biography, especially when the people were minor characters. All you could really say was what happened to them, and hope the reader would be moved by that. He likewise expected me to be able to evoke the authentic atmosphere of Cambridge in the thirties, even though the city is an alien place to me today and I wasn't even born when he was living there as an adolescent. I said you couldn't write about sights and sounds and smells if they weren't in your bones and memory. He replied that atmosphere was the most important thing of all and you weren't a writer if you couldn't create it. He was probably right, but I could only tell him that I thought atmosphere was for novels and I myself was better at irony. My writing, he also complained, was full of clichés. It was difficult to argue with that, except to say that I was doing my best not to include too many. For a time back there I became so afraid of clichés that sometimes I would even pause before writing "the" or "and" yet again. But I soon enough concluded that this was one more device to stop me writing the only kind of book I *could* write. That was the puzzling thing - in spite of his very willing cooperation in the interviews, Jack seemed otherwise to be driven to do what he could to spoil my work.

And yet he could also say, "Never ever take any notice of *anyone* when you're writing something!" This was the only advice I could accept from him, but he remained unpleased and at times furious that in spite of everything else he said I was still plodding on regardless. It was a frustrating time for me back there. As for Jack himself, well, things happened to him, unconnected with me and my boring book, that put my own minor troubles in the very deepest shade.

We did three interview sessions between April and late June, 1990, through which period I noticed no change whatever in him. On the third occasion I followed his car on a long drive through country lanes to his daughter Jenny's house at

Wilhamstead. He drove in a relaxed way, mindful that I would be in difficulties if we lost contact. Next morning, having had an overnight stay in a Travel Lodge, I again called in to return a borrowed tape recorder. He was out shopping and had left the door open for me, but soon returned and seemed entirely his normal self. Shortly afterwards I went on holiday abroad with my family. The book was going very well (at least in my own opinion) and on my return I was eager to do more interviews without delay so as not to lose the momentum. Now, though, Jack was in the middle of a hectic round of radio interviews to publicise his new novel, *Albert Rides Again*, which had just come out in hardback, and making a date for another session proved difficult. In a letter, he told me too that he was shortly to be a panelist on the BBC television Sunday lunchtime literary programme chaired by P D James and had to keep his mind free for that. Next I heard that he had flown up to Glasgow to record the show, which hadn't gone well. He had fallen out with another panellist beforehand, having failed to recognise her, and had besides been plagued by his recurrent gout so that he had had to remove his shoes - not usually a problem for talking heads on television, but the table at which they sat was open-fronted. I was naturally eager for the programme to be screened; he had been told that it was to be the first in the series but in the event it went third. Curiously, when it at last came on Jack *was* wearing shoes, perfectly normal ones. But he did behave a trifle oddly, criticising a book of stories by a guest author because none of the characters had a decent car. I had in the meantime talked briefly to him on the phone and found him in manic mood; his whole life had changed, he kept saying, though without explaining quite how. No further interview was in prospect, and for the first time my letters were ignored. Then I heard from Jenny that he had been hospitalised, diagnosed as being on a permanent "high". Apart from a hand-scrawled message from a "lunatic asylum", we lost contact. My project was completely stalled. Only months later when he sent me "Cross in Hand", a piece the national newspapers wouldn't publish which eventually appeared in *Staple*, a literary magazine put out by East Midlands Arts (with which he had connections), did I find out what had happened in that late summer of 1990. More recently he has talked to me on tape about it, at greater length.

The first thing to say is that Jack has very clear memories of what he is apt to refer to as his "lunacy" - an ironic comment on how it was perceived by others. If pressed, he does concede that he did go somewhat off the rails back then and grudgingly acknowledges that his friends and relatives had reason to be concerned. Mainly, though, he talks in terms of being a victim of misunderstanding.

Although I myself hadn't noticed anything amiss (difficult to spot of course in a man like Jack), his troubles seem to have begun some time earlier. In the autumn of 1989 he was publicising the new *Live Now, Pay Later* trilogy, published by Allison & Busby together with a new paperback of *The Trouble with Harry*. Leaving the radio station in Nottingham he was asked by someone if he had "the tape", which another person further back was calling for. Which tape was actually being referred to was never specified. Somehow the trivial incident lodged in his brain. He began to believe he was being followed - something to which he had always been a little prone, given the kind of people and organisations featured in some of his novels. In fact at that very moment he was working on *Albert Rides Again,* in which there is a plot - set in the future - to blow up the Channel Tunnel. With the excitement of the publicity round, too, one can see how his mind could have been a little fevered just then.

But the condition wasn't disabling; unlike his chronic hernia, which in spite of the surgery in the early eighties was again worse than ever. The best he could do still was to stuff his soft hat inside his truss to prevent his lower bowel leaving his stomach area and finding a new resting place in his scrotum. When that happened the situation required urgent attention;

outdoors he was in desperate trouble. From Nottingham and Pebble Mill, he travelled down to Brighton and did a radio interview there. On the street afterwards the hernia came out, and needing a toilet as well he was in real difficulties. He made his way to the beach and there dug a hole to conceal himself while he performed the complicated manoeuvre of hauling back the wandering bowel and refitting the truss assembly with the rolled-up hat inside. Relatively relaxed again, he walked back into the town, still needing a toilet. By chance he bumped into Ned Sherrin, who was in Brighton for the opening of a play. Sherrin was in a hurry and had little time to spare for a conversation with Jack Trevor Story; but all Jack wanted was to follow him to his hotel and use his toilet facilities. Sherrin was uncomprehending, and made off. Jack never did find a convenient toilet in Brighton; he suffered on the train all the way back to Milton Keynes and his own bathroom. All that was an ordeal for a man of seventy-two, but his mind was okay - except perhaps for the shadowy people behind fences, around corners, and dogging his footsteps.

The main event in London that autumn for the new reprints was a special screening of *Live Now, Pay Later* at Twentieth Century House; in attendance were survivors from the film. Jack himself was a kind of master of ceremonies and warm-up act. He spoke to the audience, introducing Liz Fraser, Thelma Ruby and others, and then announced the reading of a new short story - evidence that he was still at work and a demonstration of how his stuff sounded now, twenty-five years after the film. It was a little satire about the winds of the world, blowing this way and that and joining forces against opposing winds, written for reading, with repetition to maximise audience arousal. Unlike his reading at the *Trouble with Harry* special screening a few years earlier, this performance went down very well. I wasn't able to be there myself, but I understand he had the people in the palm of his hand. He was much congratulated later and advised to take up public talks and readings as an alternative career to writing fiction. Jack didn't in fact stay for the film itself, which he thought by now rather dated; instead he went for a drink in a nearby pub. No one seems to have held this against him, however, and the event did him no damage at all.

Allison & Busby were part of W H Allen and things were happening internally at this point which I can't comment upon except to say that in spite of the quite favourable reception for these reprints (*I Sit in Hanger Lane* was soon to follow), the prospect for Jack's *new* novels was worsening. His old friend and champion Clive Allison, with whom he had collaborated on a rough publishing schedule, was beginning to lose or vacate his position of influence so that the Jack Trevor Story portfolio was put into the hands of editor Peter Day. Despite the rumblings within W H Allen, Jack received assurances that authors' interests would be respected and remained optimistic, knowing that the only way a publisher could get out of difficulties was to sell more books. That was the theory, but eventually - and this is through into the new year, 1990 - it emerged that Peter Day too was becoming semi-detached, from an apparently disintegrating organisation. Jack agreed to put all of his manuscripts and books in the proposed schedule into his hands, taking them personally down to his house in Shepherds Bush. He noted that Day appeared to be less than thrilled to receive this delivery, and I have to say that with the deteriorating situation at W H Allen I don't know what Jack's basis was for still believing that the publishing programme might continue (beyond *Albert Rides Again*, which was already set up and close to launch). His spirits were not dampened by the visit, however; he was in buoyant mood and there now came another eccentric happening in Jack Trevor Story's manic year.

He was quite close to Broadcasting House, and feeling important in the world again, though with no money in his pocket, he decided to drop into the once familiar bar for a drink on the pretext that he had an appointment with Louis Marks (whom he hadn't seen in years). A difficulty was that he had broken his glasses. Before entering he picked up from somewhere a piece of bright green insulated wire, which he was able to use to reattach the side-piece in place of the lost little screw. He had no means, though, of cutting off the surplus and was left with an embarrassing long bright green end. Instead of trying to conceal this he decided to make eccentric use of it by fashioning it into a little but quite visible antenna. On the strength of the Louis Marks appointment he was served a pint of bitter and a double-whisky chaser and took a seat - alone but very much on show. Despite his weakness for faces and the length of time since his last visit, he believed he knew and was in turn recognised by most of the people in the bar. Soon he heard satisfying whispers: "Jack Trevor . . . Trevor Story . . . Jack Trevor Story." It was a happy moment; he was back in an old haunt and making an impression. Soon of course the barman came forward to tell him bluntly that the Louis Marks appointment was known to be a fabrication and to ask him to leave quietly. But no matter, it was mission accomplished so far as he was concerned: Jack Trevor Story was back in circulation.

There was I think only slight abnormality here; the visit to the BBC with the little green antenna was a deliberate act of eccentricity, as was a new tendency to abbreviate his speech and to involve others in his worries about being followed. It was surely all relatively unimportant; there couldn't have been any real mental disorder at that point for it was in April that he did the first of his long and entirely lucid interviews with me, which I have on tape.

Soon after this, in June, he attended Clive Allison's birthday party at the W H Allen offices, which was followed by a meal in a nearby Greek restaurant. Jack had with him a doctor friend, David Murray, but not his mate Bill Johnson, who had long experience of his sometimes unruly behaviour and knew how to defuse it. The service in the restaurant, so Jack says, was somewhat erratic. In his paranoid way he began to believe he had been selected for poor service and protested accordingly. The louder his complaints became the more determined were the waiters to ignore him, so that in the end he got scarcely any food at all. Then he *really* swore, with no Bill Johnson around to restrain him. Recognising at last that the situation couldn't be retrieved, he elected to leave, forgetting all about the friend he had brought. An American writer in London to promote his own book, who wished for other reasons to leave early, asked for a lift and was refused. Jack bounced his car over a high kerb, damaging a wheel, but this at last had a restraining effect and he managed, much the worse for drink, to drive home to Milton Keynes without further mishap. There was similar misbehaviour at other parties or gatherings around the same time, but none of it was strictly abnormal for Jack; he simply needed a close friend (Elaine, too, was evidently good at this) to make the necessary warning signs when the temperature began to rise. He has been banned from a number of pubs because of this loss of control; references to the working classes in particular are apt to set him off. I have been in pubs with him myself, besides spending many hours talking with him about his life in the flat, but have never witnessed his paranoia in action. As an outspoken socialist from a working-class background, I'm not sure how I've avoided it. We haven't even fallen out very often on the phone; our most violent disagreements have been by post.

The morning after Clive Allison's party Jack spoke anxiously to his doctor friend, who happily was reassuring about his behaviour and said he had had an enjoyable time anyway. But David Murray was privately concerned enough about his mental state to pass this on to Jack's GP in Milton Keynes, with whom he had certain professional links. Arising out of this, I suspect (Jack is hazy about it), he was invited to spend a few days in hospital for tests and observation. But it was a very low-key admittance; he took his guitar along to entertain the other patients and nurses, and tended the garden. There was no question of his being detained for long. He returned to the farm to resume work on a new book; soon afterwards he was publicising his first new novel in eleven years (*Albert Rides Again*), and preparing for the television show in Glasgow - with myself as a side irritant, trying to fix up further interviews for this book.

Besides the English working classes, Jack seems to have paranoid feelings too about the Channel Tunnel. This comes out in *Albert Rides Again,* where a mighty explosion, triggered by the Queen cutting the tape at the opening ceremony, is envisaged in which it is ripped apart over its entire length, dividing the Channel waters like the Biblical parting of the Red Sea. His new book also revolved around the Tunnel; he was writing it somewhat in collaboration with his friend Rosie Dalziel (a one-time Hampstead flatmate and like me a regular correspondent in more recent years), who lived down in Kent and was on a committee. But in Jack's book - "Uncommanded Rate of Climb" (a reference to air pockets) was his provisional title - the Tunnel was fought by more direct methods than the traditional genteel English ones of letters to the editor and such. He was going to make it an illustrated book. This was his response to Peter Day's new advice not to write any more fiction, which unless bestseller commercial was becoming very difficult to market. When he has a book to write Jack can't be stopped, and certainly not by warnings that the thing might not be published. He *knows* that, and at the time of writing seldom cares. But this time, hoping it might make a difference and equipped with a good knowledge from having observed his sons at work in Peter's studio of how to create the necessary sets, he planned to incorporate photographs to illustrate various surreal themes in the novel. The sets he began to construct from random materials to hand in combination with photographs and more solid art objects, at various points in his studio office and also, more bizarrely, outside on the roof and bonnet of his car. Certain of the sets required a "storm-washed" appearance. Indoors he got the effect he wanted by sprinkling Quaker Oats liberally around his office; outside there had in fact been rain to

194

give the desired result. All he needed was his camera, but he remembered now that he had lent it to Jackie. From his window he could see people looking at and beginning to think about interfering with the outdoor sets. In some anxiety over this he phoned and asked her to bring it over as soon as possible. Then he ran outside - naked, as he describes it - to protect his creations. The weather was very hot.

Jackie was delayed. Feeling suddenly low and a bit weepy (not an abnormal condition for him), he got in the bath, arranging a few picnic items and a glass of wine within reach for comfort. It was at this moment that Bill Johnson arrived unexpectedly. He quickly concluded, having glanced in the office, that Jack had gone round the bend and thumped downstairs to take the appropriate steps. Soon an army of people arrived with blankets. Protesting his sanity, Jack was carted off to the "lunatic asylum". He was on his own evidence a difficult patient to subdue and reconcile to the need for this drastic action.

I must let Jack speak directly here of his time as an inmate; I quote from "Cross in Hand":

> Once kidnapped . . . your witnesses appear a few at a time, with flowers and Smarties. "You must cry!" said my key-nurse. You must try to show that everybody loves you, that you have treated them badly all your life, and that now they are telling you so. "Look, he's crying. Very good."
>
> The soft-shoe shuffle of elderly lunatic life is punctuated by a telephone bell warning of the presence of wanderers or potential escapees in the shopping or garden area. There are no dogs, but whispered conversations take place, small histories are revealed . . .
>
> I do not wish to incriminate the living, but it is my bounden duty, as Lenny Bruce might have said, to prepare good though elderly people without plastic cards for futures

of gloom and despair. "Never pick one up," says Lenny,
talking about midgets. "They really hate that."

When you come out everyone wants to give you a little
dog. I think this is English. Your family are shocked at
what the place has done to you: the day-long shuffling in
the mentally subnormal carpet slippers, the side-effects of
unknown chemicals, blindness, mindless, no reading or
writing anymore, no coherent stream of consciousness.
Hopefully they see the old you with a little dog. Instead of
with heat wave hypomania.

In his more recent account on tape Jack puts the
manoeuvring to make him cry whilst asking for the forgiveness
of his loved ones at the time of his release, which was to be
preceded by a meeting with his daughter Caroline and her
husband, in whose temporary care he was to be placed. Now
Jack and Rohan have apparently never got on; he protested that
being with them would amount to an extension of his hospital
imprisonment. He might as well stay there, or preferably go
home, since he was by now technically a voluntary patient. But
he saw that good sense was going to prevail and instead of
complaining further changed tack; he asked for coins and
telephoned a television unit in Nottingham, inviting them to
come and film the bizarre family interview. They jumped at
the idea, he says, but his call had been overheard and the
filming was blocked.

I must say that missing from Jack's account of these events
is any explanation as to why Caroline and Rohan would be
ready to take him to live with them for a period of
convalescence if he was so unwilling and at the same time fit
enough now to return to Milton Keynes. They had their own
busy lives - jobs to go to - and yet he makes it sound as if they
were eager to take over the burden of being his jailers from the
hospital mainly for the pleasure of it.

But whatever the reasoning, he was taken to their home
down in Sussex irrespective of his wishes, where everyone

seems to have had a most unhappy time. So tense was the situation that when Jack lingered too long in an outside lavatory one day he emerged to find that two police cars had arrived in response to a report that he had gone missing. On another occasion he got lost on a shopping trip to Brighton (where he bought a pair of very expensive shoes with a credit card they didn't know he had) and finally had to take a long taxi ride back, whereupon Caroline quite naturally flew at him. In the hope that he might simply be allowed to leave, he made arrangements to meet Peter Day in London to discuss the publishing schedule. Here he was really testing the prison, as he refers to it, and predictably his minders didn't take the plan seriously. Instead, so as to allow Caroline to go to work, they took him to another relative who lived on a farm or small holding quite nearby. Jack now had escape one way or another at the front of his mind. He hadn't sufficient money for a train into London, but desperate to regain control of his life he simply walked away when he saw the chance, along a country lane. When he heard a car coming (Caroline and Rohan were due) he jumped down through bushes into a dry ditch and lay very still. Soon he heard car doors slamming and voices above, but he was out of sight and as time passed he became calmer and more than ever resolved to regain his freedom.

He spent two nights wandering the Sussex fields and sleeping rough, by day pretending to be a professor of botany from Leicester University, for which role he rehearsed lines of dialogue in case he should be questioned. A missing-person call had gone out on the radio, but the several police cars he saw were satisfied with his little wave and didn't stop. In his botanist role he collected berries, wild flowers and grasses from the fields and hedgerows. Eventually he came to rest in a village called Cross in Hand, where he telephoned a friend, Jim Lemmon, who lived in Maidenhead, to come and rescue him. Then he asked for a glass of water at a pub and borrowed a pen and paper to make notes on his plant collection, sitting out in the sun. He had given clear directions except for the fact that there were several Cross in Hand villages in the area, so that the rescue mission took about eight hours. Through the long day, waiting in a bus shelter in the heat and lacking his heart tablets, he began to feel ill and at last telephoned for a taxi to give himself up (Caroline lived only a short distance away; he had wandered in a great circle). A car at length pulled up and he started to give the depressing directions when he realised it was his rescuer. The taxi was coming along just behind, but they made off. After an overnight stay at Lemmon's mother's house in Dartford they drove up to Milton Keynes, where, with general agreement that further attempts to hold him under protest were pointless, he began slowly to try to rebuild his life. The precious sets had of course been dismantled and his office put back into civilised order. As for his half-finished manuscript, "Uncommanded Rate of Climb", that was missing and would never be found. But it would be some time before Jack Trevor Story was able to write again, for depression now set in.

He remained severely depressed through the autumn of 1990 and into the winter. I had done as much as I could manage of the book and believed it could never be finished. I honestly wondered if Jack would survive. Here is a letter received some time in December:

Brian:
You don't know how ill I am. I am losing everything. My driving licence most probably on Jan 8th. My feet are crippled with something, I cry with sheer sadness. I am alone here and all night, I can't smile or read or watch. There is no Christmas. You would not believe my appearance. I have not bathed for a month. Taken a bath, I mean. I dress in yesterday's clothes, shirts, vests, etc. My eyesight is a mess, close to. This letter is to make me type, though my finger ends are split. What about another book about whatever is out of the question. I do not have one

writing urge . . . Brian, my life has gone. "You are much better," my family keep saying, to get rid of me. I am obsessively depressed. I envy you your life, your energy, your money . . . I keep slipping into bed with my shoes on. This is the last furlong before the big jump, I would think.

Jack at Xmas 1990

And in January came a kind of general circular:

There is nothing to write about. Summer of 1990 suddenly died. There has been no writing since then. The events of August lay flat in my memory, without colour or spirit. I have no urge to write about it. My life since my writing died is like something that happened to somebody else. Even reading other writers no longer interests me. I have died. Something has destroyed the joy in my heart.

One night I dropped my dentures into a mug of hot cocoa. I cried tears. It seemed to sum up everything. Perhaps the approach of death . . . What has happened to my happy, creative life? I do not know. I count my drugs. The disaster, whatever it was, has something to do with drugs and medicine. Tonight I will swallow a lithium tablet. Lithium is a mood stabiliser - perhaps it keeps me depressed and stops me writing . . .

That letter arrived on a Saturday morning. My wife is a pharmacist, so I asked her about lithium. She asked what else he was taking so I phoned to find out. He sounded a little better on the phone. His list of drugs included a diuretic, and his remarks suggested that his fluid intake was insufficient, because of worries about swollen ankles. My wife said this could lead to lithium poisoning, which could mean very severe depression indeed. Soon afterwards I heard that he had stopped taking the drug, on his own decision. There was no immediate relief from the melancholia, however, or so he remembers it.

But I do recall an arrangement to meet in February that had to be cancelled because he had been taken into hospital with a kidney stone.

The pain of that, amazingly, was the final cure. He emerged from the experience "like a fairy dancing out of a Christmas parcel". Recovery was rapid; he resumed writing, beginning a sort of autobiographical fantasy story with the title "Shabby Weddings". Soon I began to receive odd fragments and chapters in the usual way. And as before I found it difficult to be of much help as a literary confidant and critic since I couldn't see where the whole work was heading. Jack was bringing famous people into his own adventures - themselves fantastic - so that you couldn't help wondering what they might have to say about it if the book were published. Running though "Shabby Weddings" as well is an invented "umbrella wedding" - a marriage of true souls with a girl from his past which transcends the real relationship of his life. But I have been too preoccupied with my own difficult project to give this new work the kind of attention it deserves. Coping with the ordinary circumstances of Jack's life is task enough for me.

There was a change in Jack "post-holocaust": he became more professional in his general approach to selling his work, and more critical of what I was doing - definitely unwilling now to be treated as a figure of fun. My early chapters are flippant in tone, reflecting my view of him in the early days as something of a professional eccentric. I once said to him that I was finding it hard to keep a kind of mocking tone out of the book. He hasn't forgiven me that. Once you say something wounding to Jack it can never be *un*said. I have tried to explain that "mocking" was the wrong word; "amused" would be better - but he won't buy that, any more than he will let me off the hook with the argument that that tone was appropriate in the early stages, since when the book has I hope become more serious.

Because of his new pride in his position and reputation, this year has been far more frustrating for me than those first easy

months in the spring of 1990. Several times I have responded
to angry letters about the book with heavy sarcasm, and even
insults of my own, threatening to abandon the project
altogether. At least twice I have actually done that, once
stuffing all of my reference material into a cardboard box to
dump in my loft and forget about. Had it not been for the
staunch support of Jack's old friend and pen-pal Mrs F V
Dunstall ("Floss" to her friends) down in Sevenoaks, to whom I
have been sending the manuscript a chapter at a time, I would
not have been able to pick myself up. Here are a few lines
from a letter of Jack's in June:

> Your inaccuracies are deliberately contrived to show me as
> stupid and non-literary and you as cultured . . . vicious
> rubbish. You want the butcher boy image . . . Like all
> second-rate writers, going for cliff hangers, or an ironic tag
> to end your chunks on. Never mind it is rubbish . . . *You*
> thought I *should* be thinking that in order to give your rotten
> writing some rationale. You are the worst writer I have
> ever read and God damn it, you are beginning to creep into
> my new autobiography . . .

How did I climb back from that? Well, I happened to be close
to Milton Keynes one day on business and called in to ask the
straight question: did he want the book to continue? The
straight answer was yes. And so we have limped on, scarcely
having a cross word when we are together, but fighting all the
time by post, and now and again on the phone, too. Somehow
I have weathered this buffeting and stuck grimly to my task,
bringing the biography at last to within sight of completion.

I must close this chapter with the appalling news that Jack Trevor Story has been found dead alongside his worktable (Thursday, December 5th, 1991) with a piece of paper in his typewriter.

Chapter Twelve

JACK TREVOR STORY EXPLAINED

Writing in the sixties in "A Soft Word to the Gravedigger", William Saroyan said this:

> . . . Nor is it unusual for any writer to read that he is
> steadily declining. One might say it is unavoidable, because
> nothing is so convenient to the inept critic than to point out
> that the writer under consideration started out fairly well
> but quickly went to pot . . . There are specialists on this
> subject, and of course they prefer the writer to be dead.
> But let the writer still be hanging on and it makes trouble
> for the specialist. He can dig a grave, but he can't put a
> live man in it . . .

And here is Jack Trevor Story, writing in the eighties about Saroyan's poignant short story *Dear Baby*, which had made such an impression on him back in 1944:

> Imagine my stupid little eyes starting to blink . . .
> "Listen. After the fight I send you some girls. We'll
> have a party. Are you there? Are you okay?"
> "I'm okay, Sam."
> Now I was crying. It was not just the girl dead and
> the boxer's future therefore empty, any new triumph
> meaningless. It wasn't that so much. It was the general
> insensitivity of everybody you ever knew in your whole
> life . . .

Two sobering texts for this final chapter.

It is death of course that changes everything. Makes you see clearly now. Crystallises your thoughts. Causes you to ask how you could have been so unbelievably stupid, blind, lazy, and all the rest of it. An ego has to be extinguished.

When I saw Jack Trevor Story for the last time on Wednesday, 27th November, I said something like this at one point:

"I hope you won't mind this and I'm sorry, but the natural ending for this book is to leave you here at Stacey Hill Farm, fighting off carers and holding grimly to your independence, aged seventy-four, with winter coming on again . . . I'm sorry, but that's the most effective ending . . . I hope you won't mind . . ."

He had just shown me blood on the wall at the bottom of the long steep wooden staircase down which he had recently fallen, close to heavy plumbing on which he had banged his head, resulting in concussion and a brief spell in hospital. He complained of dizziness since the accident, but his mind seemed as clear as ever. He had nothing to say in response to my remarks, though, and I may even have repeated them, rearranging the words a little to make them more palatable. I thought that as a writer he would be able to put his personal feelings aside and agree with me that what mattered was to do the right thing in terms of art. Never mind the hellish winter he might be facing, isolated in the cold farm flat, always worrying if his car would start next time, having sometimes to walk to distant shops in biting winds, trying to believe in his work still when through the summer, with damaged eyesight (a legacy, he said, from his lunacy period), he had worked so hard with so little result in terms of how the stupid world judges these things.

And it wasn't as if I didn't *know,* that I hadn't the capacity to understand that so long as a writer was still at work, still doing his best, that was all the world could ask of him. He might be out of fashion, or luck, but if he was writing still he remained successful in the only way that ought to mean anything. I *knew* all that; I was the one who had selected "A Soft Word to the Gravedigger" for inclusion in *The New Saroyan Reader*. And all the time on that last visit, out in the open, was the collection of Saroyan's essays in which I had first read the piece.

Jack Trevor Story had many gravediggers, as every man has, and certainly every artist. My own excuse can only be that I had absolutely no expectation that he would soon die. He had had his hernia miraculously fixed in the summer and, the dizziness apart (and it was easy to believe that that was going to improve), seemed in better shape physically than for some time. And his mind and spirit seemed in good order, too. There seemed no reason, in other words, why I shouldn't *be* a little insensitive. Jack wasn't a man to handle with kid gloves.

"Are you all right?" people were always asking him lately, in that nervous voice we reserve for the old and infirm. He really couldn't stand that. Once, back in March, I was sitting with him and Bill Johnson in the Crown at Stony Stratford, on bar stools. This was before his hernia surgery, and Jack looked to be uncomfortable. I asked him is he would be better on an ordinary chair with a back rest - realising instantly that I had said the wrong thing and that he would store it up against me. He never forgot anything; never really forgave.

Our last afternoon together began badly. He insisted on playing an old tape for me of Maggie talking to another Scottish girl, a friend or relative, and himself playing his guitar in the background, taking no part in the conversation. I had actually heard it before and was a trifle impatient because I had just driven a hundred and fifty miles after a morning's work and wanted to get as much as possible out of the visit for my direct needs. But he persisted, and of course the right tape had to be found, and the right place on the tape, all taking some time. What he seemed to want to demonstrate was the extent to which music and guitar playing were central to his existence. In my book I have pretty much ignored his musical life because he was after all famous as a writer, not a musician - and anyway I have felt unable to cope with it, besides not having the space.

"But it's my whole life," he said. "You've missed my entire life!"

Now had I not been immune to such remarks it might have been a devastating charge. I had done the three-hundred mile round trip six or seven times and had spent every available lunch period for more than a year scribbling out this book, typing the stuff up in odd moments of privacy at home because I can't bear any disturbance when I'm writing (and typing is for me the final revision). So far as I was concerned it had been a near super-human effort, all done with little expectation of publication; but now suddenly, casually, critically, I was being told that the thing couldn't possibly be any good because I had missed out his music, and music filled his entire time and being. So what did I say, listening to Maggie and friend chattering in their Scottish accents, with someone fooling on the guitar, rather obtrusively, in the background? I said this:

"It sounds to me like a child, irritated and bored by adult conversation, who seeks attention by making a noise of its own - pitched not quite to drown the talk, but certainly to spoil it."

After that the wonder is that we did any recording at all. But as I've said, it was unknown for us to have heated words when we were in each other's company. I knew, therefore, that my latest faux-pas would only be stored away; that our taped conversation, the reason for my long drive, would not be affected.

My plan from an early stage has been to include in this final chapter the transcript of a direct interview with Jack, in which we would explore what seemed to me a number of paradoxes in his life. Well, after going out on a brief shopping expedition in the late afternoon we opened a bottle of wine and actually did that interview. I had even brought along a list of these paradoxes. With a little editing, mainly of my own voice, this is how it came out:

DARWENT: The first of these paradoxes is your admitted shyness, which would seem to be in conflict with a strong desire and drive in your early life for fame. Which you pursued very energetically.

STORY: No, I don't think there is any conflict. I think it's a complementary thing. People with extrovert ambitions are introverts. If they have ambitions of any sort - to be a film star, or a tap dancer, or stand-up comic - they're likely to be very shy people who go away and commit suicide in Australia. Because it seems to me they're so intensely tied up in themselves that it becomes a terrible strain. So I don't think there is any conflict there. The same in all the arts, really.

DARWENT: So you're saying the two things are complementary. Most people would see then as opposites.

STORY: Can I interject there? That's what they say, isn't it? I've done chat shows. BBC2 said to me would you like to do your own chat show? What guests would you like? So I said Ronnie Wolfe and Mike Moorcock. Mike is not *very* forthcoming - he's very nervous. And he's an extrovert. Well, look at him. There he is playing his guitar, and he wears a cowboy hat. He's a cowboy Buffalo Bill. You put him in front of a camera, with a chat-man talking to him, and he's suddenly polite. I daresay I'm the same.

DARWENT: So are you saying that a person who is shy and who admits to being shy, as you do, in fact is more capable than an extrovert, who in reality is even shyer than your are?

STORY: I think that's roughly right, yes . . . When I got to my feet at Harrogate a few years ago - A J P Taylor was next to me, Stan Barstow, Keith Waterhouse, Monica Dickens, all the Penguin writers were there. I got to my feet talking tofour hundred people and said, "I'm absolutely terrified. My head's shaking - it always does when I'm nervous. The back of my neck twitches. I've been like this all week and I've written the speech six times. I've got them all here." I took the six speeches out of my pocket. I gave them the irst line from each of the six speeches. By the time I'd got through doing it everyone was laughing and the atmosphere was relaxed.

DARWENT: It's almost as if the extrovert is unprepared for these moments. When confronted with the reality of microphones and audiences and so forth the extrovert can collapse completely. Whereas the person who admits to shyness can make himself ready.

STORY: I think that's true. I like to make people laugh, to break the ice. There's always some ice to be broken. But I've noticed when I've sat in the chair and interviewed other people, the people you're relying on to make everybody laugh, they don't do it because they're very shy people. This

extrovert-introvert thing - as you say, you
can't pin it on people. I mean, you take
A J P Taylor. He was at that dinner that
day. He's a quiet little man, isn't he? But
isn't he a good speaker? And everybody
listens intently, don't they? More so than to
the people who make jokes . . . I think
being believable is the answer. I think if
you're believable people are ready to listen
to you, and they go quiet.

DARWENT: So you think the extrovert is really putting
up a facade all the time?

STORY: I think so. Because I do that sometimes, and
I'm not happy with it.

DARWENT: It's apt to collapse?

STORY: Yes, and people are quick to detect it as
well.

*

DARWENT: The next thing is, you admit to being a
physical coward - as in the incident with Bill
Johnson on the river. In your childhood you
were not very active in physical things,
sports and so on. And yet in your life and in
your writing you have been very
adventurous - certainly in your romantic life.

STORY: Impulsive. Not adventurous, though.

DARWENT: Taking a chance, taking a *big* chance, with
your women, with your writing . . .

STORY: Jumping in at the deep end they call that.

DARWENT: In other parts of your life you are not at all brave.

STORY: Physical parts, you mean?

DARWENT: I've noticed it in your dealings with publishers and editors.

STORY: I've never been frightened of anybody. But I have been inhibited. That's quite a different thing. I'm inhibited by anybody who's got a university accent. Now sometimes I can get over it, luckily. I know how to get over it because I've got street-cred. I didn't know anything about street-cred till I met my last little wife, because you get something from everybody. But if all they've got is the accent, I think I can't even talk to them. If they're wearing a *tie* it puts me off.

DARWENT: Don't you see there's anything in this - physical cowardice, and on the other hand in your writing and romantic lives you've taken wild gambles? I mean, I don't know it you've had any trouble with rivals?

STORY: What sort of cowardice do you mean when it comes to my love life, then?

DARWENT: No, you're adventurous there, as in your writing. I'm just trying to draw a contrast between that and other parts of your life.

STORY: You won't find in me any cowardice when it
            comes to talking to publishers and editors,
            because I'm fully aware of how famous I
            am. At a *Punch* lunch I would say, "Who
            are those geezers down the other end of the
            table?" They'd be the board. So I've always
            got this awareness of being Jack Trevor
            Story, and that's a very famous name. But
            that doesn't stop me being inhibited on a
            personal level if I'm talking to somebody
            who is over-choked with education. It's just
            the fact that he's not being natural. I'm not
            frightened of them, but I can't talk to them.
            I'm not being myself . . . When it comes
            to the physical side of adventures - that day
            on the river I really went to pieces. I
            thought we were going to be drowned, and
            the thought of being drowned terrified me.
            I'm not afraid of aeroplanes getting into
            trouble, as last August, going up to
            Glasgow. . . . I'm not afraid of heights.

DARWENT: But you do in a more general sense admit to
            being physically a bit cowardly.

STORY: I wouldn't get into a fight, I agree with you
            there. I'd rather run than fight.

DARWENT: What about the risk of your involvement
            with women who belong to other men?

STORY: I've never done that in my life. I'm
            religious about that. I'd never have anything
            to do with anybody who belonged to
            somebody else. Unless they haven't told me
            about it. I think it's a bloody *awful* thing to

do. I was so hurt by it and I know other
people are hurt by it, that I couldn't do it.

DARWENT: So the superficial view of you is wrong - that
you were always on the make as far as
women were concerned.

STORY: No, not always. There's always an
exception that proves the rule. When I was
in charge of Special Products Tests I had
working for me an engineer who brought his
wife in - very sexy, very glamorous. She left
me a message under my green baize, a little
letter - every engineer had his green baize
which you put your tools on. It didn't
matter that you were the boss. I used to
send her husband up to the north of England,
just to give myself a few nights with her.
That was an exception, because it was what
she wanted.

DARWENT: That's the exception?

STORY: Well, it is, because it's always been on my
conscience.

DARWENT: But the conventional view of you would be
that you were doing that all the time. What I
am trying to put up here is the conventional
view, against the reality.

STORY: I'll tell you the reality, and I think Elaine got
it right. She said, "For God's sake don't
have a one night stand with anybody - that's
ten years of your life gone. You can't have
anybody without staying with them for at

least five years." And she meant it. It's
absolutely true. Once I've had sex I feel I've
got something permanent.

*

DARWENT: Next I've got vanity. You strike me as
being in some respects a vain person. But
you've always been willing to show your
worst - or non-flattering - side, as for
instance in that photograph in the *Sunday
Telegraph* a couple of years ago, which is a
very interesting photograph but not really
flattering.

STORY: But that's the one that's in the National
Portrait Gallery.

DARWENT: Yes, it's a terrific photograph.

STORY: Why don't you think it's flattering?

DARWENT: It's a terrific portrait, a terrific photograph . . .

STORY: You mean it hasn't got a collar and tie on?

DARWENT: No, it certainly isn't flattering in any
conventional sense. You're not there
attempting to look as - you know, you think
of the *vain* man in front of the mirror, fixing
his tie and combing his hair.

STORY: I said as soon as she got here, "What shall I
wear?" She said, "Nothing. You're perfect."

DARWENT: Yes, but she's a professional photographer. And it's a terrific photograph, as I keep saying.

STORY: And I'm proud it's in the National Portrait Gallery.

DARWENT: Absolutely, yes. I'm not saying anything against that.

STORY: You remind me of Bill Johnson, when you say that. He said, "Oh, Jack, in the *Sunday Telegraph*. Did you see it? It was terrible. For God's sake don't ever use that photograph." I said, "Bill, I've got a lot of them - in the National Portrait Gallery." He aid, "Oh no, no. You want a crushed hat. You want Humphrey Bogart." I said, "No, that's the way *you* see authors. You want Hollywood Jack Trevor Story. With a crushed hat and a suave expression and a striped tie." And the family think, "Oh, dad . . . "

DARWENT: All I'm saying is that it isn't compatible with vanity in any conventional sense.

STORY: Oh, I think it is. I see what you mean.

DARWENT: What about this Ugly Agency you belonged to? You take a certain delight in offering yourself for public display through an agency like that, even though you're also somebody who would spend time in front of the mirror making himself look presentable and attractive.

STORY: The Ugly Agency never struck me as an
             ugly name . . . I think I know what you're
             saying. Being in the Ugly Agency is a
             vanity, you see. Otherwise you're saying
             that vanity is being good-looking. And that's
             ridiculous. Vanity is trying to look the way
             you are.

DARWENT: So vanity can extend to being ugly as well as
             being handsome?

STORY: Oh, yes.

*

DARWENT: Now I've got here love and sex, which
             we've already touched on, and which I don't
             want to spend long on anyway. With you it's
             a difficult thing to understand, because your
             life seems to be devoted to the pursuit of
             love, essentially, in an almost sexless kind of
             way. And yet you've been sexually active
             with many different women.

STORY: Well, I think I told you this before. The
             people who are bad at sex have most
             children. I think that really sums it up.
             Because even the thought of a french-letter,
             in my head, puts me off.

DARWENT: You make this strong distinction between
             love and sex.

STORY: I don't want to separate them. But I fall in love with people without legs, really. What I see is the eyes and the face and the hair, and I'm in love. The idea of a bed would ruin it, kill it. When it comes to desiring somebody I love, I can't do it. So we never have any sex, because the love would go. So then I fuck her sister, or her best friend.

*

DARWENT: Coming to your writing, another apparent conflict is between your training as an engineer - a very precise discipline - and your writing. Especially your *fantasy* writing.

STORY: It's just the opposite.

DARWENT: You'd think you would have wanted to escape from that sort of discipline . . . but I'm conscious that that wasn't true.

STORY: Anybody who writes about Picasso says he couldn't have done his later painting if he hadn't been a first-class conventional artist first . . . Unless you're a mathematician, you can't write at all. You can't do *anything* in the arts unless you're a mathematician. You've got to know the Quantum Theory, which quite simply is that as soon as you touch something it changes . . . I think there's a discipline in engineering, which unless you've got that discipline you can't skid around on fantasy skates. You've got to know where the reality is.

DARWENT: One of the things that seems to distinguish you from your contemporaries is that you have continued to develop as a writer, right down to the present day, really. Whereas so many writers - of all periods - have made their name with a certain style and rather stayed with it.

STORY: Well, they have to, because they make a living out of it. You can't make a living if you change. Kingsley Amis is still writing the same book. John Braine was still writing the same book.

DARWENT: Your style has developed - advanced, if you like - and the books - beginning with *Hanger Lane*, I would say, and certainly *One Last Mad Embrace*. . .

STORY: I don't think the books are important at all But I think that I'm a writer's writer, and all my most satisfying reactions have been because I'm a writer's writer.

DARWENT: For anyone who's interested in you, the ones from that period - from *Hanger Lane*, then *Little Dog's Day* and *The Wind in the Snottygobble Tree* . . . I'm really trying to establish that you recognise that your style was still developing and you weren't in a fixed style, writing the same book, like the others.

STORY: I don't know why it bothers me, but it does. The word is not develop. You're not getting better. The best book is the first one you ever did. A virgin is the best creature there is in the world.

DARWENT: What's the word, then - instead of develop?

STORY: I don't know . . . It's a growth . . . No, growth is wrong as well . . .

DARWENT: Well, it's developing. It's building on what you've already done.

STORY: No, no it's not. Quite the opposite. It's - thank God - managing to get rid of what you did last time. I'll never do that again, I made a terrible mistake there. You can't say that's developing . . . No, perfection comes from absolute innocence. If you get really close to innocence, you're there. And it only happens so rarely.

DARWENT: So what do you see that you're heading towards, then, in your writing?

STORY: Oh, you're not heading towards anything. You're just trying to stay close to innocence. I think innocence is the only word for it.

DARWENT: So it's a bit like Picasso again. He said he was all the time trying to learn how to draw and paint as a child.

STORY: Yes, that's absolutely it. Wanting to get rid

of cleverness. Smartness. True poetry is
innocence . . . Otherwise, you see, you get
the feeling that the guy thinks he's getting
better and better, when really he's losing it.

DARWENT: What about this tendency you have to put off
the ordinary reader? Deliberately.

STORY: Oh yes, I agree with you. That's perfectly
true. Because *I* have an awful job reading
Albert Rides Again.

DARWENT: Individual sentences seem most important to
you.

STORY: Yes, I gathered from certain writers and
critics that my whole interest in writing is in
the perfect sentence. Now, what the sentence
says I don't give a fuck about. I never have.
And people said, "I don't agree with what
you said in the *Guardian* yesterday." And I
said, "What was that, then?" I didn't know
myself what I'd said. If they said it was a
marvellous piece, that's terrific. Because
what they're looking at is the *writing* then.
It doesn't matter a shit what you say. And
I've always felt like that.

DARWENT: Like painting again. A lot of people look at
a landscape, and all they're interested in is
where it is. For me the painting itself is what
matters. So is there a parallel with writing?

STORY: What they call it is form and content. And
I'm interested in form, but not in content.
Which is why when I pick up a book I open

it anywhere, and I'm away. I don't care
what came before and what comes next. But
I'm never ever conscious when writing that
I'm regarding this as separate from that or
that from this. I just write the way I write,
really. It's instinctive.

DARWENT: What about morality?

STORY: I had two or three parsons used to write to
me. Preachers. Vicars. Asking if they
could use passages from *Live Now, Pay
Later* in their sermon next week, or their
speech to their youth club. I used to write
back to say they needn't ask me those sorts
of things. But they said, "Oh, I do ask you,
because they make such very good moralistic
points. So I'd like you to know I'm doing it,
and which parts I'm using." And I thought that
was rather nice, really. So when I was reading
The Urban District Lover in the pub
yesterday - he's talking about when Jesus
saw the city, he wept. I thought that was
precisely right. That's the first time Albert
realised abortion was wrong. When Christ
saw the city He wept was all the things that
we do all the bloody time, and Albert
particularly - until suddenly he realised he
was doing it . . . Those were the things the
parsons wanted. Now, people who have a
different view of me - my son-in-law - say,
"I don't believe you! A vicar writes to you
to ask if he can use a bit of one of *your*
books, in *church*? Don't talk fucking
rubbish!" Because if you write about the sins
of humanity, and the vulgarity of humanity,

they think the book's about the sins of
humanity and the vulgarity. It's not. It's
about the guy who *suffers* from the sins and
vulgarity . . . I can't *stand* vulgarity. If I
say fuck, I *know* I've said it. And I make
sure it's in the right place . . .

Leaving the flat that last time I told Jack for Christ's sake to
be more careful on the stairs. He wished me luck with the
book, as he always did, and a safe journey home, and love to
the family. He never missed any of that. I felt guilty because
once again we had scarcely talked about his own book,
"Shabby Weddings", which I knew he had been writing almost
as a parallel exercise, hoping in a vague sort of way that the
two might be published together. I sincerely hope they are.

Two or three days later, seeking only a little more information
about his trip to California in the early eighties, I telephoned
Jack at my usual mid-morning time. He had told me in a letter
that the information was all in a *Guardian* piece, specially
commissioned, which he *knew* I had; but the fact was that I
didn't have it - couldn't remember having seen it. I had meant
to ask him about the trip on my visit, but with so much else to
cover I had forgotten. Several times on the phone I had had a
less than friendly reception. My visits in a sense spoiled his
whole day, because he couldn't concentrate on anything else if
he was expecting someone - especially me, I fancy. So I think
he expected to cover everything then, or at any rate in letters,
which *didn't* interfere with his day. Phoning, therefore, was a
bit of an imposition, on top of all the other contact. Now,
though, the project was almost complete; the stuff about the
California trip was really the last information I was going to
need. So I picked up the phone.

As I had expected and rather feared, Jack's mood turned to
irritation when we had got through the pleasantries and he
realised why I had called. I told him what I understood of the

trip, which wasn't much. "You know almost nothing about it, do you?" he said, in what sounded like amazement. (One of my great difficulties throughout has been his notion that I ought to know all about his life already - shouldn't need to ask. That has been the basis of most of his angry criticism of factual errors in my work.) But he consented to run quickly through the facts I needed (now incorporated in Chapter Ten) while I desperately scribbled notes. Then - and this was pretty unusual on the phone - he did turn nasty. Out came all his stored up hatred of what I was doing - my motives, my refusal to consider major re-writing, my hopeless failure to recapture his golden Cambridge years, my deadness to his musical life (I was the only person he knew in whose presence he didn't play his guitar), and above all the sneer in everything I wrote, in my every utterance - my mocking tone, my obscene plan to end the book leaving him an isolated old has-been. "Why not end it in New York?" he said; for he had been approached in connection with some video talks which might indeed have meant a trip to America again. I said I was perfectly ready to end the book on a positive note if I could; I would like nothing better. Then I got some of my own stuff in about all the time and effort I had expended and how he ought to be thankful he was dealing with someone of my integrity, who wasn't simply trying to use him. How I had several times, knowing how he felt about it, tried to abandon the project, only to be encouraged to carry on by none other than himself. And how disappointed I was by his attitude when I had hoped all along that my book might actually do him a bit of good, insulting as that must now sound. But I couldn't keep this up and began to stumble over my words, whereupon he did a mocking echo of this stumbling.

"You're an arsehole, Brian!" he said, with feeling, before hanging up.

I wasn't going to pick up the phone again, so I did the only other thing I could in the circumstances to vent my own feelings - wrote a letter. This sounds terribly childish, but it should be remembered that ours was a mainly postal relationship; we had known each other for years by letter, before ever meeting. So I was simply following a routine procedure, and my anger was in truth a little synthetic. But I did what I could to turn the sneering charge against *him*. It seemed to me that he had always looked down his nose at my every interest and enthusiasm. He had mocked my humour, too, by seldom laughing at anything I said, or for that matter wrote. Then I attempted to rebut his paranoid idea that I was setting myself up in the book as somehow his superior. I said sarcastically that I felt myself to be second-rate in most departments of my life, so if he was going to call me an arsehole, please make it a *second-rate* arsehole. Something like that - I hardly know what I said because I didn't keep a copy.

Next day a BBC Radio producer phoned me in connection with a programme he is making about Jack. He had enough to say to give me an excuse to write to Jack again - which again was typical of these rows. This time I said soberly and sincerely how sorry I was he disliked the book so much, but I was at a loss to know - since he knew my limitations and couldn't bear sycophancy - what kind of biography he had expected me to write, or to be capable of writing. And then for some reason - maybe a premonition of some sort, I don't know - I felt moved to add a word about how much I admired his brave stand against old age, infirmity, carers and a number of other things, including death itself.

Always in a day or two a letter would come back, commonly making no reference to what had last been said. Once, after a similar row, he wrote in a puzzled way, "I seem to have irritated you." But no letter ever came this time. Instead, about a week later, a man at the *Times* phoned. He had the job of writing Jack Trevor Story's obituary.

April 1990 - December 1991

Index

Page